Introduction to VersaCAD®

RICHARD E. COOPER
DIABLO VALLEY COLLEGE

Merrill Publishing Company
A BELL & HOWELL INFORMATION COMPANY
Columbus Toronto London Melbourne

Published by Merrill Publishing Company
A Bell & Howell Information Company
Columbus, Ohio 43216

This book was set in Palatino.

Administrative Editor: Stephen Helba
Production Coordinator: JoEllen Gohr
Cover Designer: Russ Maselli

This book is designed to provide tutorial information about the VersaCAD computer program. Every effort has been made to make this book as complete and accurate as possible.

The information is provided on an "as-is" basis. The author or publisher shall have neither liability nor responsibility to any person or entity with respect to any loss or damage in connection with or arising from the information contained in this book.

Library of Congress Catalog Card Number: 89-61509

International Standard Book Number: 0-675-21164-6

Printed in the United States of America

1 2 3 4 5 6 7 8 9--93 92 91 90

TO STUDENTS

Students who will be using this book are potential drafters, not programmers. Many will have had no previous experience with computers, although they will have some drafting background. With this in mind, I have avoided rewriting the *Versa-CAD Manual*, so students won't be overwhelmed by new vocabulary or by a complete overview of the program. Instead, they'll find that this book teaches through hand-on experience. Each chapter introduces several ideas followed by exercises at the computer that make the ideas concrete.

TO INSTRUCTORS

Even if instructors have no computer-aided drafting (CAD) experience, they'll be able to use this book, learning VersaCAD at the same time their students do. The heart of the book is its exercises, many of which require the student to produce and submit plots. Even with little or no CAD experience, instructors will be able to grade submissions based on their knowledge of manual drafting.

The first ten plot submissions require approximately twenty-four hours to complete. These plots give students in a beginning manual drafting class some useful experience with computer-aided drafting, and can be easily accomplished even in classes where computer access is limited. If the instructor is experienced with computer-aided drafting and can introduce students to each chapter in this book, the same exercises could be covered in perhaps two-thirds the time. To complete all plot submissions would require approximately one hundred hours.

SYSTEM SETUP

To do the exercises students will need an IBM XT, AT, or PS/2 computer or compatible with a minimum of 640K memory; a hard disk; a math coprocessor; an EGA or VGA color monitor (a monochrome monitor could be substituted to complete most of these exercises); a mouse (a digitizer could be substituted); and a 6-pen A-size plotter with the following pen colors:

1 black, narrow

2 red

3 green

4 blue

5 orange or tan

6 black, broad

The drawing instructions can be easily adapted to any other plotter arrangement. This book covers VersaCAD Design versions 5.2, 5.3, and 5.4. Please note that the Macintosh edition of VersaCAD is not covered in this book.

PARTIALLY COMPLETED DRAWINGS

As with manual drafting workbooks, it is sometimes convenient for the student to simply complete a drawing that has already been started than to draft an entire drawing from start to finish. In this book are references to a number of such partial drawings, which are on disk and can be obtained from the publisher. Since the disk is not copy protected, its contents can be transferred to other CAD stations at the teaching site.

ABBREVIATIONS

Four directory abbreviations are used in this book. Directory names differ at different VersaCAD installations.

Abbreviation	Meaning	Usual Directory
F:	The directory containing VersaCAD's 2D FONTS, DRAW, LIB, and CUSTOM subdirectories	C:\VCAD54\V2D
G:	The directory containing VersaCAD's 3D SCENE subdirectory	C:\VCAD54\V3D

| H: | The user's home directory (the directory from which the user executes VersaCAD) | B: |
| I: | The directory containing the partially drawn author (or instructor-added) drawings | C:\VCADEX |

A technician familiar with DOS can add these abbreviations to the batch file that executes VersaCAD (for example, SUBST I:C:\VCADEX). Alternately, the user can use the full subdirectory names instead of the abbreviations whenever the abbreviations are indicated.

ACKNOWLEDGMENTS

I wish to thank the following people who reviewed the manuscript and contributed many creative suggestions: J. David Alpert, Rancho Santiago College, Santa Ana, California; Thomas Boronkay, University of Cincinnati, Cincinnati, Ohio; Felicitas Dzierba, Texas State Technical Institute, Amarillo, Texas; Dennis Kerns, Ivy Technical College, Gary, Indiana; Martin Samolsky, Manhattan Technical Institute, New York, New York; and David Wendt, Western Kentucky University, Bowling Green, Kentucky. Their efforts were appreciated.

I am also grateful to the many students at Diablo Valley College whose penetrating questions and astute perceptions directed the development of this book.

The author extends his thanks to the people at Merrill Publishing, particularly Barbara Duffy whose timely suggestions made the publication a reality.

Without the enlightening criticisms, constant encouragement, and infinite patience of my wife, Tazuko Cooper, this product would have remained in its infancy.

About the Author

Richard E. Cooper is an engineering instructor at Diablo Valley College, a community college in Pleasant Hill, California. He obtained his master of engineering degree from the University of California at Berkeley. His background is in programming, computer hardware, and drafting. Some of his programming output has included a word processor, a COGO compiler, and an extensive set of graphics routines that allow CAD output from BASIC, FORTRAN, and Pascal programs.

He has directed the development of a thirty-station instructional CAD lab at Diablo Valley College, which uses AutoCAD®, CADKEY®, and VersaCAD® software. He has consulted with both schools and industry in the development of on-site CAD lab facilities and student training programs.

He emphasizes easy-access CAD labs, hands-on training, one student per station, and the integration rather than the separation of computer-aided drafting and traditional manual drafting.

CONTENTS

CHAPTER 1

Getting Started

OBJECTIVES

- *To develop a mental picture of how a computer operates for students with no previous computer experience.*

- *To begin to use directories, files, and an operating system.*

- *To learn how to format a disk.*

- *To use VersaCAD for the first time.*

CHAPTER CONTENTS

Getting to Know Your Computer

Files and Operating Systems

Your First Experience with VersaCAD

GETTING TO KNOW YOUR COMPUTER

Hardware

Hardware is the set of units (devices) associated with a computer system. The following list gives the necessary units of any computer system (diagrammed in Figure 1.1):

Input units: A keyboard, a mouse, a digitizer (and so on)

Output units: A CRT (cathode ray tube) screen, a printer, a plotter (and so on)

Memory units: Main memory, disk memory

CPU: Central processing unit

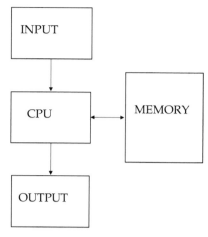

Figure 1.1

Software (Programs and Data)

Software is information that is stored and used by the computer system. Main memory stores two types of information: programs and data. A **program** is a set of computer instructions. **Data** are information that is either keyed into the computer or developed from the execution of the instructions. The **CPU** is the device that executes a program, fetching then executing one instruction at a time from main memory until all the program's instructions have been executed.

An instruction usually requires the CPU to create, change, or move data. For example, if the numbers 2 and 3 are to be added together as a part of the execution of a program, main memory must contain the 2 and 3 in the data area and the addition instructions in the program area (see Figure 1.2). A simplified translation of the addition instructions to the CPU follows:

Move the 2 from main memory to the arithmetic logic unit (the ALU is a subunit of the CPU that performs arithmetic and logic operations).

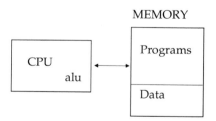

Figure 1.2

Move the 3 from main memory to the ALU.

Signal the ALU to add the two numbers it is holding.

Store the ALU result back in main memory in the data area.

Move this result from main memory to CRT output.

Questions

1. Name the four main hardware units of a computer system.

2. What are the following letters abbreviations for: CPU; ALU; CRT?

3. What does the CPU do? The ALU? The CRT?

4. Define the following: hardware; software; program.

5. Main memory contains both programs and _____.

Disk Storage

Information can be stored outside main memory on disks. A **floppy disk** is a paper-thin disk sealed in a nonremovable covering that protects the disk from dust, dirt, and the oil from your fingers. The covering has a window that exposes the disk to read-write heads. When inserted into a disk drive, the disk twirls around within its protective covering. Floppy disks come in two common diameter sizes, 3½ and 5¼ inches. When a 3½-inch disk is outside its drive, a metal slide covers its window. The window on the 5¼-inch disk is protected by placing the disk in a paper envelope.

A **hard disk** is a thicker, higher-quality disk that is usually not removable from the computer. Its read-write speed is perhaps ten times faster than the read-write speed of a floppy.

Disk capacity is measured in bytes, or more accurately, in kilobytes or megabytes (1 kilobyte [kb] = 1000 bytes, 1 megabyte [mb] = 1,000,000 bytes). A **byte** is a storage location unit used to measure the size of information. One byte of storage is required to store one character. The name JOE, for example, would require three bytes. A typical elementary **CAD (computer-aided drafting)** drawing might require 10kb of disk memory for storage.

Data are stored on the disk in concentric rings called cylinders. Depending on the disk, information may be placed on one or both sides. Disks are labeled as SS (single sided), or DS (double sided), as shown below:

Disk Size	Label	Capacity
5¼"	SS/SD	120kb
	DS/DD	360 kb
	DS/HD	1.2 mb
3½"	DS/DD	720 kb
	DS/HD	1.4 mb

Common hard disk sizes are 20, 40, or even 100 mb.

Higher quality (and more expensive) disks can pack information more tightly. Disks might also be labeled as SD, DD, or HD (single, double, or high density). For your application, you must use the right size and correctly labeled disk. CAD users often use DS/DD.

FILES AND OPERATING SYSTEMS

A person buying a computer system must purchase hardware, an operating system (system software), and other programs (application software) such as VersaCAD. Software is purchased on disks along with a manual that describes how to use the software.

A **file** is a location on the disk where information is stored. Each file has a unique name.

A **directory** is a file of filenames. When information (a program or data) is saved for the first time on disk, the user gives it a filename, which is added to the directory. The directory can be displayed on the CRT screen at any time to see which files currently exist on the disk.

An **operating system** is a program that manages input/output activity. It allows a user to store, retrieve, examine, rename, and delete information on a disk. It also moves programs from the disk to main memory so the program can be executed.

Microsoft's Operating System

The Microsoft Corporation, a software company, developed and sells a disk operating system that is used in most personal computers. This operating system will be referred to as **DOS** (**disk operating system**). A user can key in over 100 different commands to DOS; however, for most applications a user only needs a handful of these.

Booting the System

Sit at a computer station and do the following:

1. Notice how many drives your system has. A typical arrangement might be an upper drive (A drive), a lower drive (B drive), and perhaps a hard disk drive (C drive).

2. If the CRT monitor is off, turn it on.

3. If the power to the CPU is off, turn it on (look around for the power-up switch). Caution—rapid on-off toggling of a power switch to electronic equipment could produce surges that may harm part of the circuitry. Always wait five seconds before retoggling a power switch. If the power is already on, press the [control-alt-delete] keys all at the same time to simulate powering up.

4. Wait about thirty seconds for the screen to display a drive prompt (for example, A> or B>). This thirty-second process is called "booting the system." A relatively short program called a "boot program" has been burned into the main memory to remain even when the power is off. This permanent memory is called **ROM** (**read only memory**). The boot program instructs the CPU to make certain diagnostic tests upon the system to verify that its components are in good working order. It then instructs the CPU to move the DOS operating system from a disk (usually the hard disk) into main memory. DOS then begins to execute. When you finally see the drive prompt on the screen, the DOS operating system will then be ready to receive commands from the keyboard. Your first command to DOS will be to format your workdisk.

Formatting

A disk is formatted by executing a program called format. The format program's job is to create **sectors** (set up storage locations) on your blank disk so that information can later be placed in these sectors. Key in the three commands below (be sure to include the colons), pressing the key marked [enter] after each command.

Command	Comment
C:	Remember to press [enter] to end a DOS command. This command makes the current drive the C drive.
FORMAT B:	After you key in FORMAT B: and press [enter], the FORMAT program will start executing and you will be prompted to insert your disk. With the read-write window in first and the label right side up, insert the disk into drive B all the way until it bumps the back. Then for a 3½-inch disk, push slightly down to seat it. For a 5¼-inch disk, latch the door. Formatting takes about thirty seconds. When asked to format another, key in *no* and press [enter].
B:	This command makes the B drive the current drive. You work from the B drive.

The formatting process should now be complete.

Using DOS Commands

Type the commands that follow. Be sure to press [enter] to end each command.

Command	Comment
B:	Makes the B drive the current drive.
CLS	Clears the screen.
DIR	At present there are no files in your directory since you have just formatted your disk. DOS will react accordingly.
DIR C:	This command will show you a list of files in the directory on the C drive, which were placed there previously.

COPY C:\GREET B:	Use a backslash (\) not a frontslash (/). Copies the file GREET from the C drive to your B drive directory. (The GREET file contains the following message: GREETINGS! Welcome to the greeting file.)
DIR	Notice that the file GREET is now in your directory on the B drive.
TYPE GREET	Type the word TYPE as well as the word GREET. This command tells DOS to display the contents of GREET.
COPY GREET JILL	Copy the contents of file GREET now in your directory to a new file JILL.
DIR	Note there are now two files in your directory.
REN JILL MARY	Rename the JILL file to MARY.
DIR	Notice there is no longer a JILL, but there is a MARY file.
TYPE MARY	Same contents as old JILL file, of course.
DEL GREET	Delete your practice file.
DEL MARY	Delete MARY also.
DIR	Note GREET and MARY have been deleted.
[ctrl-alt-del]	While holding down the [control] and [alt] keys, press the [delete] key. Pressing these keys will reboot the system. (Try it.) This allows you to start all over when you get hung up on the computer and don't know what else to do. Rebooting does not change the disk contents, but *will* erase the main memory contents.

Please note that computers with only one floppy disk drive will now have a "Non-system disk" error displayed. No problem. Just remove your disk and depress any key to recover from the error.

That's it. Allow five seconds of inactivity so you know your disk is not being accessed by the system. Remove your disk and walk away. If you're pretty sure the computer will be used within two hours, leave it on. Otherwise, turn off the CRT and the computer. You may wish to repeat this exercise two or three times to get a better feel for DOS file activity.

Filenames and Commands

A filename may have up to 8 characters; however, there must be no space between characters. It also can have up to three extension characters preceded by a period, for example, LINES.2D or T3-7PQ.ABC. In addition, a filename may also be preceded by a drive name followed by a colon and a backslash. Some examples of these variations follow:

DEL BILL   Deletes the file BILL from the current directory.

COPY C:\GREET B: Copies the GREET file from the C drive.

TYPE A:\GEORGE.PAS   Displays on the screen the contents of the GEORGE.PAS file.

DOS does not distinguish between lowercase and uppercase letters. DIR, dir, Dir, dIr all mean the same.

Questions

1. Name four DOS commands.

2. What is a file? A directory?

3. What happens when you *boot* the system?

4. What does it mean to *format* your disk?

5. Do you need to format your disk every time you use the computer? (No! You'll destroy all the files stored on it!)

6. The commands DIR and TYPE both require DOS to display something on the CRT screen. What is the difference between these two commands?

7. Is there any difference between a capitalized command and an uncapitalized command? What is the difference between DEL and del?

8. Where is the directory located: *(a)* in main memory *(b)* in the CPU *(c)* on the disk *(d)* at the CRT or *(e)* by the phone book?

YOUR FIRST EXPERIENCE WITH VERSACAD

Sit at a station, insert your disk in drive B, then type the following:

Command	Comment
VCAD	Remember to depress the [enter] key. You are now beginning to execute VersaCAD.
D	Select the *2D Drafting* option. (Once in VersaCAD there is no need to press the [enter] key. DOS commands require it, but VersaCAD commands don't.)
	Select a menu item by typing in one of the uppercase letters shown. Start by typing the letter A, then L to begin drawing a line. Moving the mouse to the right moves the graphics cursor into the drawing area. Depress any button on the mouse to "pick in" one endpoint of the line. (*Pick* means to press the mouse button.) Move the mouse until the tracking line is where you want the line to be, then pick the second endpoint of the line.

Experiment for awhile with the various menu items. Try drawing a few lines. Draw a line with an arrow on the end. You cannot select the arrow option until the first point of the line is set. Draw other objects, too.

Occasionally an excessive movement of the mouse makes the cursor jump off the screen. Subsequent mouse movement may move the cursor still further away from the graphics area so that you've lost the cursor. Not to worry—there is a solution: Depress both buttons on the mouse simultaneously to automatically move the cursor to the bottom left of the screen. Although the cursor is still off the graphics area, a short movement of the mouse to the right will bring it back.

After experimenting, return to DOS by typing *Q* repeatedly to return you to the DRAFTING menu; then type *X* (*eXit*) along with *Yes*, to return you to the main menu. From there, another *X* will return control to DOS. (You will know that DOS is in control when you see the familiar B> prompt.) You can now remove your disk and walk away. No need to turn the system off.

Next-Time Station Usage

The next time you wish to use VersaCAD, do the following:

1. If the CRT monitor is not on, turn it on.

2. Turn on the power-up switch.

3. Insert your disk in the B drive.

4. Type VCAD to execute VersaCAD.

5. Press *D* for *2D Drafting*.

CHAPTER 2

Lines and Rectangles

OBJECTIVES

- *To create, save, and plot a first drawing.*
- *To draw lines and rectangles.*
- *To delete objects previously drawn.*

CHAPTER CONTENTS

Fundamentals

VersaCAD

Lines

Drawing: Line-Point

Exercise: Border

Rectangles

Drawing: Rectangle

FUNDAMENTALS

Records

A **record** is a set of data created by VersaCAD, usually consisting of the name of a geometric figure together with properties associated with that figure, such as coordinate positions, line width, and color. When an object is first created and displayed on the screen, data pertaining to this object are also placed in a record in the data area of main memory in order to allow VersaCAD at a later time to redisplay this object. If the user selects the *sKetch* menu item, VersaCAD blanks the graphics display area, then uses the records to redisplay the drawing.

The Workfile

Initially, CAD records are saved in main memory where they can be speedily retrieved when needed. However, records in main memory are saved only as long as the computer is turned on. If there is a power failure, a user who has spent a number of hours on a drawing could lose all of it. This condition would be a disaster if main memory were the only storage place for CAD records.

Fortunately, data can be stored magnetically on disk and retained even with a power failure. To avoid loss of work, many CAD programs require users frequently to stop drawing in order to save on disk the work they have developed so far. In contrast, VersaCAD automatically copies the most recent records to a file on the hard disk called the workfile (see Figure 2.1). In fact, VersaCAD updates the workfile every time you type *Q* (*Quit*) to exit a command. When power is restored after a power failure, records in the workfile are automatically moved back into main memory when you execute VersaCAD, so that you can continue drawing, losing only those records since the last *Quit*.

Saving and Retrieving a CAD Drawing

When you leave a station, you can copy the drawing (actually, the contents of the workfile) to a floppy disk, which you can

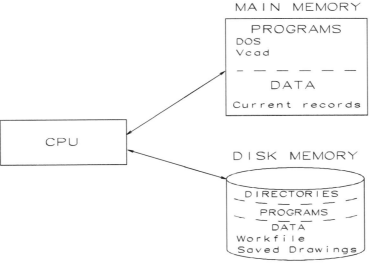

Figure 2.1

take with you. At a later time, you can execute VersaCAD and have it copied from the floppy disk back into the workfile on the hard disk.

VERSACAD

When VersaCAD first executes, it presents the user with a list (menu) of eighteen items. You can select a menu item by moving the mouse or by keying in the uppercase letter shown in a menu item. Each selection method has its advantages and disadvantages. If you are familiar with the keyboard, keyboard selection is probably best. Try both methods, then decide.

Each menu item is a command to the CAD program to perform some operation. With each menu item selection, a new submenu is displayed. No command may be selected unless it is currently displayed as a menu item.

Quit and Escape

The user can return to the previous menu by selecting *Q* (*Quit*) or by depressing the [escape] key. With [escape], all objects that have been drawn using the current menu item are erased from the drawing. With *Quit*, the objects remain part of the drawing and the workfile is updated.

Mouse Button Equivalent

Sometimes when trying to locate the cursor precisely, pressing a mouse button inadvertently moves the cursor slightly. Keying in a star [*] character is equivalent to pressing a mouse button. Try it sometime.

VersaCAD Vocabulary

Primitives are relatively simple geometric figures that are used in combination to form more complex figures. VersaCAD uses ten primitives: point, line, arc, circle, rectangle, polygon, ellipse, curve, text, and multiline. These primitives are selections within the ADD menu.

A **symbol** is a combination of primitives joined in a way that allows it to be used as though it were a primitive. An arc and a circle are primitives. An egg isn't. But an egg can be drawn as a series of connected arcs, saved as a symbol, then drawn with a single menu selection as though it were a primitive. Symbol usage will be postponed until primitives are well understood.

An **object** is a primitive or a symbol.

A **marker** is a plus sign (+) placed in the geometric center of an object. Markers are especially convenient for drawing circle centers. A marker menu item is selectable at appropriate times, usually *after* the first point for an object has already been picked.

A **guide** is a line (guideline) drawn temporarily as a drawing aid, then later erased. A guide menu item is selectable at appropriate times.

A **template** is a temporary object drawn with dotted lines, later to be erased or drawn in solid, or partly erased and partly drawn in solid. A template menu item is selectable at appropriate times, usually after the first point for an object has been picked.

LINES

A line is drawn by picking two end points, points 1 and 2. Some options are allowed after (and only after) point 1 is picked. The menu items are described below.

Menu Item	Comments
Connect	When point 2 is picked it will automatically become point 1 of the next line. Connected lines will be drawn. (This is the default value, which means that *Connect* is in effect whenever you begin VersaCAD.)
Detach	The tracking line is erased. A new line can be drawn disconnected from the last line.
Single	Single (unconnected) lines can be drawn.
Erase	Erases previous point picked. If no previous point, quits to main menu.

Features:

Arrow	Displays an arrow at the head of the tracking line.
Marker	Displays a midpoint marker on the tracking line.
Template	Displays the tracking line as a template (dotted) line.
	A feature is removed if it is selected again before point 2 is picked; otherwise it becomes a part of the object when point 2 is picked.

Constraints:

X-axis	The tracking line becomes an X-line. Cursor movement modifies length.
Y-axis	Tracking line constrained to Y direction.
Rotate	Tracking line constrained to R-axis direction (see Figure 2.2). This direction is a multiple of the rotation angle, which may be preset to

---

■ Menu Commands

Add›Line›Connect
Single
Erase

Pick point 1

Add›Line›Connect
Detach
Single
Erase
Arrow
Marker
Template
X-axis
Y-axis
R-axis (rotate)
Free

Pick point 2

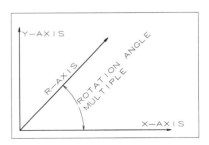

Figure 2.2

any value. Each time the R key is pressed, the
tracking line direction increments by the
rotation angle amount.

Free   Unconstrains the tracking line so its head is
                 at the cursor.

Deleting an Object

The ADD menu is used to draw an object. In contrast, the
MODIFY menu is used to change an object once it is drawn.

When you select the MODIFY menu, the last object drawn
begins to blink. If the cursor is not in the graphics area, blinking
is suppressed. To see which object is currently selected, move
the cursor into the graphics area.

An object must be blinking before it can be modified. To make
each object blink in turn, you can use the forward [>] and
backward [<] keys. Often a quicker way to make an object blink
is to select *Find*, then pick any point on the desired objects. If
you select *Delete*, the blinking object will no longer be displayed. However, it is not deleted from the workfile. If you
wish, you can again display the deleted object by selecting
Undelete. Currently deleted objects are discarded when you
save your drawing on disk. A saved drawing does not contain
deleted items. *Quit* returns you to the DRAFTING menu.

■ Menu Commands

Modify›Find
    > (forward)
    < (backward)
    Delete
 	
    Undelete
 	
    others

❏ DRAWING: LINE-POINT

Note: The drawing for this exercise can be found in Figure 2.3.
Draw what is shown in the figure, but do not draw the reference letters or the border.

1. Execute VersaCAD by typing VCAD.

2. Select *Drafting*.

3. Guidelines: Select *Add›Guides›Y-axis*. Use the mouse to
move the cursor. Pick point A. Repeat to set guide at the other
point A.

4. Connected lines: Select *Line*, then pick point B. Select

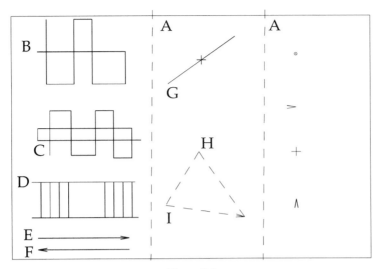

Figure 2.3

X-axis. After the first X-line is drawn, the line automatically changes to a Y-line. Draw the eight connected lines shown.

Select *Detach*, pick point C. Select *Y-axis*. Draw connected lines. Select *Detach* to move to point D.

5. Single lines: Select *Single*, pick point D.

Select *X-axis*, then draw two lines. Select *Y-*, draw eight lines. (*X-, Y-* options do not automatically change when *Single* is selected.)

6. Arrow, marker, template: Pick point E, select *Arrow*, draw line.

If a menu item appears all uppercase, the feature associated with that menu item is activated. For example, *Arrow* changes to *ARROW* when selected, and an arrow is placed at the head of the line that is currently being drawn. As long as *ARROW* is all uppercase, any line drawn will contain an arrow head. If you again select the *ARROW* menu item, it will revert to lowercase and subsequent lines will not contain an arrow head. Draw the next line but start from the right, picking point F last—otherwise, the arrow will point in the wrong direction.

Pick point G, select *Free* to remove X-lock, then select *Marker* to display a marker at the midpoint of the line. Draw the line.

Whoops! The arrow is still on the line. Select *Erase*. Select *ARROW* to remove the arrowhead, then pick point 2.

Pick point H, select *Template*. Select *Single* to toggle back to connected lines. Select *Marker* to remove the marker. Draw template lines, selecting *Arrow* then *ARROW* at the appropriate times.

7. Points: *Quit* back to the ADD menu, select *pOints*. (Select with the letter *O*, not *P*. *P* is used for *Polygon*.) Draw the points, arrowheads, and markers on the right, selecting the necessary menu items.

8. Sketch: Select *sKetch* (use *K*) to redraw the drawing. Note that guidelines have disappeared. They are not redrawn.

9. Saving your drawing: Select *Filer>Save>All*. Name your drawing LINES, and it will be saved on the B drive. Select *Quit>Quit* to return to the DRAFTING menu.

10. Plotting your drawing: Select *Output*. Turn plotter on, making sure that it's connected to your station. Insert plotter paper. At your station, select *Plotter*, then use the default values by pressing [enter] each of the three times a plotter question is asked.

11. Submitting your drawing: After the drawing is plotted, *Quit* to the DRAFTING menu.

Verify: Select *eXit>Yes>eXit*, to return to DOS. Key in DIR to verify that your drawing has been saved as LINES.2D. (The screen will show the filename as LINES.2D. Note that VersaCAD refers to the file as LINES and DOS refers to it as LINES.2D.

Submit: Pencil your name at the bottom right corner of your plot and submit it for grading.

The Reference List

When the user keys in VCAD and selects D (*Drafting*), the DRAFTING menu is the first menu displayed. The Reference List at the front of this textbook displays the menu items in the DRAFTING menu together with the submenu for each DRAFTING menu item. Make frequent use of this reference list as an aid in understanding VersaCAD's menu structure.

❑ EXERCISE: BORDER

Note: The drawing for this exercise is shown in Figure 2.4.

1. Border: Execute Vcad and select *Drafting*. Select *Filer›dRive›I:›Get›$BORDER›dRive›B:* (Files beginning with $ are instructor-drawn partial drawings stored in a directory designated as *I:*)

2. Modify: *Quit* to the DRAFTING menu, then select *Modify*. Remember that an object must be blinking before it can be modified, and the cursor must be in the graphics area for an object to blink. Test this by moving the cursor over to the menu area. No blinking. Now move it back to the graphics area to see an object start blinking. However, it may be the wrong object. Use the forward [>] and backward [<] keys to make other objects blink. When SMITH, JOE blinks, select *Delete*.

Select *Find* and place the cursor over any point on the tilted line just after the word JOE. Pick it to make it blink. Select *Delete*. *Quit* to the DRAFTING menu.

3. Title: Place the cursor near the middle of the drawing area. Select *Add›Text*. Key in your name, using capital letters, then press [enter]. Move the cursor until your name is in SMITH, JOE's old location and pick. Again press [enter] to finish add-

Figure 2.4

ing text. Draw a new vertical (not tilted) line just after your name.

4. Save border: Select *Filer›Save›All›BORDER›Yes* to save the new BORDER for future use. Leave the $ off the name.

5. Plot for your records but do not submit. Exit VersaCAD. End of exercise.

RECTANGLES

To draw a rectangle, select *Add›Rectangle*, then select the method for defining the rectangle.

<table>
<tr><td>**Menu Item**</td><td>**Comment**</td></tr>
<tr><td>*Corners*</td><td>Pick a corner of the rectangle. A tracking rectangle is displayed whose opposite corner is at the location of the cursor. Pick the opposite corner of the rectangle.</td></tr>
<tr><td>*Three pts*</td><td>Each point becomes a corner of the rectangle. This method is usually selected when points 1 and 2 already exist on the drawing. Point 3 is determined by the distance of the cursor from line 1–2. (See Figure 2.5.)</td></tr>
</table>

■ **Menu Commands**
Add›Rectangle›Corners *Three pts*

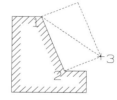

Figure 2.5

❏ DRAWING: RECTANGLE

Note: This drawing is shown in Figure 2.6.

1. Execute Vcad.

2. Rectang: From VersaCAD's DRAFTING menu, select *Filer› Get›BORDER›Quit*, then change the title to RECTANG. Add guides 1, 2, and 3 to help size your drawing. Add DISTRICT CT in the top left corner, then draw a rectangle around it.

3. Copy: *Quit* to the DRAFTING menu, select *Modify›Copy*, and copy a rectangle where SENATE is to be. Place the rest of the rectangles by eye, then *Quit*.

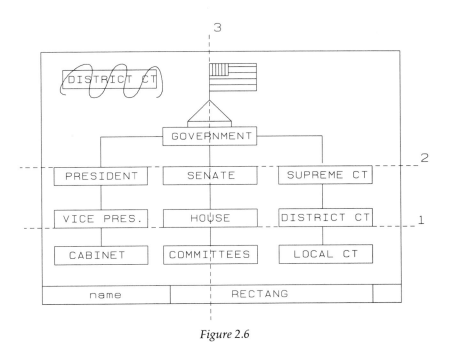

Figure 2.6

4. Finish: While still in *Modify*, delete the top left DISTRICT CT along with its rectangle. Finish the rest of the drawing, then select *sKetch* to remove guides. Select *Switches›Fatlines› Yes›Quit* to increase the thickness of the lines.

5. Save as RECTANG, plot, and submit.

CHAPTER 3

Circles, Arcs, and Polygons

OBJECTIVES

- *To add arcs, circles, and polygons to a drawing.*
- *To preset object properties.*
- *To explode a polygon from a single object to its many legs.*

CHAPTER CONTENTS

CIRCLES

A circle is drawn by picking a center location and then selecting a radius, or by picking the two end points of a diameter.

Menu Item	Comment
Center/radius	Pick center point 1 (see Figure 3.1). Select the radius with cursor or keyboard.
›Cursor	Move cursor until tracking circle is desired size. Then pick the radial point.
›Keyboard	Select *Radius.* Key in a radius value. If before picking the radial point, *Radius* is reselected, a different radius can be keyed in. Pick the final radial point.
Diameter	Pick diameter endpoint 1. (See Figure 3.2.) Select the other diameter endpoint with cursor or keyboard, in a manner similar to selecting the radius (described above).
Three pts	Pick three noncollinear points; a circle will be formed containing these three points.

Markers

The circle center can contain a marker by selecting *Marker* after point 1 is picked. However, if the circle is already a part of the drawing and a marker is desired, then some effort is required. Do the following from the DRAFTING menu: *Modify›Find the circle›Properties›Misc›Marker›Yes›Quit›Update›Quit›Quit.*

ARCS

To draw an arc, either three points or a center and two points are required.

Menu Item	Comment
Three pts	Pick arc endpoints 1 and 2. Select point 3 by tracking the arc to the desired shape with the

---

■ **Menu Commands**

Add›Circle›Center/radius
Diameter
Three pts

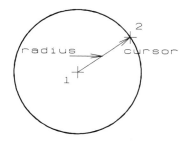

Figure 3.1
CENTER/RADIUS

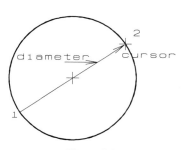

Figure 3.2
DIAMETER

■ **Menu Commands**

Add›Arc›Three pts
Center/2 pts

cursor or by keying in a radius value.

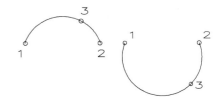

Figure 3.3
CURSOR

›Cursor   Move cursor. Tracking arc appears with cursor as inner point 3 (see Figure 3.3). Pick desired arc.

›Keyboard   Select *Radius*. However, two points and a radius determine four arcs, not one (see Figure 3.4). To select the desired arc of the four arcs (labeled A, B, C, and D), begin moving cursor at *r* and slowly move to *s*; each arc will be displayed in turn. Pick the desired arc when it displays.

Center/2 pts   Pick center point 1. Pick endpoint 2. Move cursor to point 3. If the wrong-direction tracking arc is displayed rather than the desired arc, select *Direction* (see Figure 3.5). The default direction is counterclockwise. Pick point 3.

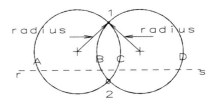

Figure 3.4
KEYBOARD

❏ DRAWING: ARC-CIRCLE

Note: This drawing is shown in Figure 3.6.

1. Execute Vcad. From the DRAFTING menu, retrieve your border drawing with *Filer›Get›BORDER*.

2. Select *Filer›dRive›I:›Merge›$ARCS›Yes›dRive›B:* (At this point, if you had used *Filer›Get›ARCS* instead of *Merge›ARCS*, your border would have been erased.) Note that student drawings are stored on a floppy disk on the B drive and instructor drawings are stored on the hard disk in a location abbreviated as *I:*.

3. *Quit* to the DRAFTING menu.

4. Draw circles and arcs in the proper rectangle area as instructed in Figure 3.6. Don't include the instructions as part of the drawing.

5. Car: In the lower right rectangle, finish the car and place the label SUPA KUPA CAR on the car's side using *Add›Text*. When

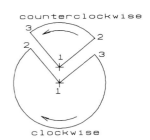

Figure 3.5
DIRECTION

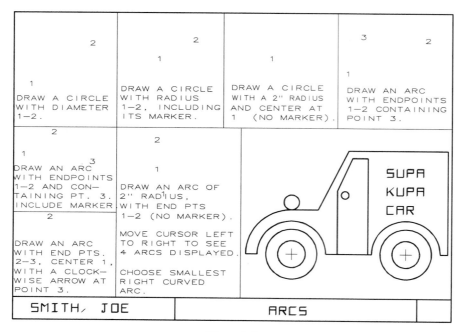

Figure 3.6

you want to quit adding text, press [*enter*]. (Don't type in *Q* to quit—VersaCAD will treat the *Q* as text.)

6. Select *Switches›Fatlines›Yes›Quit* to thicken lines.

7. Save your work under the name ARCS. (Leave off the $.) Plot your drawing and submit.

PROPERTIES

When a CAD program is instructed to draw an object on the screen, it must also create a **record** of information about the object. This record must contain enough data for the program to be able to redraw the object at a later time. When a drawing is saved, the picture itself is not saved; instead it is these data records that are saved.

A record consists of the name of the object, geometric information, and the object's properties. The following are examples of two records:

■ **Menu Commands**

Properties›lineStyle
          lineWidth
          Density

          Color
          Pen
          Text

          others

Record Number	Object	Geometry	Properties
1	Line	X1,Y1,X2,Y2	lineStyle, Color, lineWidth, . . .
2	Circle	X1,Y1,radius	lineStyle, Color, lineWidth, . . .

When an object is first drawn, its properties are obtained from default or preset values. Properties can be preset by selecting *Properties* from the DRAFTING menu. Once a property is preset, all new objects added to the drawing will be given that preset property until the user changes it. For example, preset the color to red and every line drawn afterward will automatically be red.

Properties is included in the DRAFTING menu. (To preset a property from any other menu, press the [F6] key. After the property is preset, *Quit* returns you to the menu displayed before you pressed the [F6] key.)

Menu Item	Comment
lineStyle	Eight line styles are available (see the Reference List on the inside front cover for an illustration of these line styles). Line styles are preset by choosing the appropriate number. For a solid line choose no. 1.
lineWidth	If *lineWidth 3* is selected for a line and if *Switches›Fatlines* is preset to *Yes*, then the line will be plotted more than once, with each line offset from the previous line by $\frac{1}{64}$ inch, making the lines appear as one thick line. The screen will also display the line as a thick one. If *Switches›Fatlines›No* had been preset, then all objects would display and plot with *lineWidth 1* regardless of their line width setting.
Density	Lines are displayed on the screen using only one density. On the plotter, however, a line with density 3 would be drawn three times, each line directly over the other with no offset. Although density can be useful if the plotter pen is running out of ink, it might be better to change pens.

STD	FONT	sample	1
BLOCK	FONT	sample	2
SLANT	FONT	sample	3
SIMPLEX	FONT	sample	4
DUPLEX	FONT	sample	5
TRIPLEX	FONT	sample	6
ITRIPLEX	FONT	sample	7
IDUPLEX	FONT	sample	8
GRKSPX	ZOΞΥ	ταυπμε	9
GRKCPX	ZOΞΥ	ταυπμε	10
GOTHIC	FONT	sample	11
ENGLISH	FONT	sample	12
MATH	∩⊃⊂∪	↑≡≅≈∼≤	13

Figure 3.7
VERSION 5.4 FONT SAMPLES

Color   Color is selected by number (see the Reference List).

Pen   Pens are selected by number. In a multipen plotter the pens may be different colors and different pen widths; you'll need to examine the plotter-pen carousel to determine the color and width of each pen.

Text   The height, width, font, and spacing of characters can be preset. Font refers to the form of the letter; VersaCAD version 5.3 has three fonts: standard, block, and slanted, but version 5.4 added many more (see Figure 3.7).

POLYGONS

In VersaCAD polygons refer to regular polygons—all sides are equal. (To draw a polygon with unequal sides, select *Add> Lines.*) A VersaCAD regular polygon may have from 3 to 180 equal sides.

An imaginary circle (which will not be displayed) is used to draw a regular polygon. To **inscribe** the polygon within this

---

■ **Menu Commands**

Add›Polygon›3 sides
4
5
6
others

circle, choose a radius from the center of the polygon to one of its corners (see Figure 3.8). To **circumscribe** the polygon about this circle, choose a radius from the polygon center to the midpoint of one of its sides (see Figure 3.9).

After selecting *Add›Polygon*, select the number of sides, then pick the center of the polygon. The following submenu will display to help the user pick point 2:

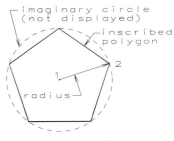

Figure 3.8
INSCRIBED

Menu Item	Comment
X-axis	Constrains the radius line to the X-axis.
Y-axis	Constrains the radius line to the Y-axis.
Rotate	Constrains the radius line to the R-Axis, whose direction is a multiple of the rotation angle, depending on the number of times R is pressed.
Free	Frees the radius line to follow the cursor.
Inscribed	This menu item is uppercase by default, and the polygon will be drawn inscribed in the imaginary circle. If you select this menu item, it becomes lowercase and the polygon is drawn circumscribed.
Radius	Instead of picking point 2 at the cursor location, select *Radius*, then key in a radius value for the imaginary circle.

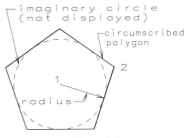

Figure 3.9
CIRCUMSCRIBED

EXPLODING A POLYGON

To modify only one line of a polygon, you can explode the polygon. Although it won't look any different on the screen, it actually becomes a series of connected lines rather than a single object. For example, to delete one side of a triangle, use: *Modify›Find triangle›Explode›Find side›Delete›Quit*.

A line is exploded about its midpoint so that it becomes two lines. However, exploded arcs and circles become a bunch of squiggles, a misery to erase, so avoid exploding these.

■ Menu Commands
Modify›Find›Explode

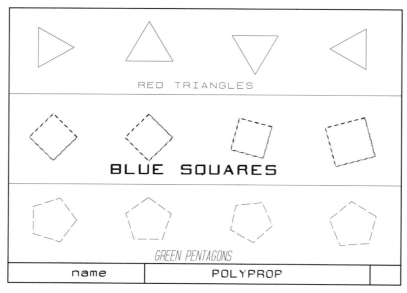

Figure 3.10

❑ DRAWING: POLYGON-PROPERTIES

Note: These drawings are shown in Figure 3.10.

1. Execute Vcad. Use *Filer›Get* to place BORDER on the screen.

2. Use *[F6]›Width 1*, then *Add›Line›Single* to separate the drawing into three areas horizontally. Use *Add›Guide* to separate into four temporary areas vertically.

3. Red: Use [F6] to preset the following properties: *Color red, Width 1, Text 7⁄16" high and wide, Font 1*. Press [enter] for column and row. (Columns and rows are not used here.) Add the text *"RED TRIANGLES"*.

Use [F6] to make the rotation angle 30 degrees. Angles are measured at the center of the polygon from the +X-axis counterclockwise. After the center is picked, press the R key the correct number of times to draw the regular triangles so that a corner is at 0 degrees, then 90 degrees, 30 degrees, and 60 degrees. Use the [F5] long-cursor key to help line up centers.

4. Blue: Use *Properties* (instead of [F6], for variety) and change preset values to *Short-dash lines, Color light blue, Pen 4, Width 3, Text 11⁄16" high and wide, caps, Font 2*. You may wish to press [F5] to return to short cursor for awhile.

Add the words *"BLUE SQUARES"*, and draw the regular squares so that a corner is at 0, 90, 30, and 60 degrees.

5. Green: Use [F6] to preset some properties to *Long-dash lines, Color green, Pen 3, Width 1, Text ¼" wide, ¾" high, caps, Font 3.* Add the text *"GREEN PENTAGONS"*. Draw the regular pentagons so that a corner is at 0, 90, 60, then use *F6›Rotation* to draw the last one at 22 degrees.

6. Use *sKetch* to remove guidelines. Use *Filer* to save as POLYPROP.

7. Plot (remember *Switches›Fatlines›Yes*).

On your plot, notice that the width and line choices (width 3, dashed lines) for the squares give poor results. There will be a way to correct this (later). Also notice that the triangles on the *screen* are red because *Color 2* was selected in Step 3 above. However, on your *plot* they are not red because *Pen 2* was not selected. On your plot near the triangles make a comment in pencil, "Should be red but Pen 2 was purposely not selected," then submit.

CHAPTER 4

Drawing Aids

OBJECTIVES

- *To use various aids in creating a drawing.*
- *To use the snap concept to set the cursor at precise locations.*
- *To modify the properties of an existing object.*

CHAPTER CONTENTS

Drawing Aids

Window

Exercise: Window

Units

Exercise: Increment-Rotation

Snap

Exercise: Snap

Fatlines

Changing the Properties of an Existing Object

Exercise: Changing the Border

Drawing: Snap

DRAWING AIDS

T-squares, triangles, protractors, french curves, templates, and scales are some of the drawing aids used by traditional drafters. Correspondingly, *Window, Snap, Increment, Rotation,* and *Fatlines* are among the drawing aids used by computer-aided drafters.

WINDOW

Window is selected from the DRAFTING menu. With *Window*, the user can define a rectangular area within the drawing that is to be displayed in the graphics area on the monitor screen.

■ Menu Commands
Window›In
Out
Base
Full
Pan
others

Menu Item	Comment
In	Magnifies by defining a rectangle in the current graphics area. After the rectangle is selected, the contents of the rectangle are enlarged to fill the graphics area. As a consequence, there will be objects in the drawing outside the rectangle that will not be displayed in the new graphics area.
Out	Reduces the contents of the graphics area so that more of the drawing can be seen. After the user defines a rectangle in the current graphics area, the contents of the current graphics area are reduced to fit within this rectangle, allowing room for other objects to fit in the new graphics area.
Base	Displays that portion of the drawing that was displayed before windowing.
Full	Displays the drawing so that all objects in the drawing are as large as possible but still fit within the graphics area.
Pan	Moves the window up to one window away from the currently displayed window. The pan can be in any direction.

❏ EXERCISE: WINDOW

1. Execute Vcad. Select *Filer›dRive›I:›Get›$WINDOW›dRive› B:* The file $WINDOW is a drawing of objects including a triangle within a rectangle.

2. Select *Window›Full* to have the drawing fill up the screen.

3. Select *Base* to resketch the drawing with the original base. Again, select *Full* and *Base* to see the effect.

4. Select *In* and draw a window (rectangle) around the small triangle. Window in on the sign the man is holding. Window in on the exclamation point. Window in on the period in the exclamation point. Within the dot above the *i* is a somewhat sensual symbol.

5. Select *Out*, then draw a window in the upper left corner. All objects in the drawing area will be redrawn within this *Out* window. Try *Out* a few more times.

6. Select *Base*, then window in on any one of the figures but do not pick the second point of the window yet. Instead, alternately select *Move* and *Scale*, moving the cursor to get the feel of how these menu items execute. Select *Place*, move cursor, then select *Move*. Finally press the [escape] key.

7. Select *Base* to sketch the original drawing. Select *Pan*, which moves the drawing window; pick the approximate center of the graphics area, then pick the center of the circle. The circle will move to the center of the graphics area. Try panning a few more times.

8. Select *Base*, then try drawing the following lines as well as you can without windowing.

_ _

9. Quit window; then add a single line from point 1 to point 2. Add line 1-3. Add line 4-5. Add line 6-7 (points 6 and 7 are the midpoints of the legs of each rectangle). Add line 8-9 (point 8 is at an intersection and point 9 is on the circle at a location that makes 8-9 pass through the center of the circle).

10. Window in on the various lines you drew to view the apparent impossibility of placing lines exactly where you want them. Whereas windowing in and drawing a line will place the line more accurately, further windowing in will still display the placement errors.

11. You will return to solve this placement inaccuracy problem after the next exercise.

12. End of exercise.

Pixels

A CRT screen is coated with a phosphor substance that glows when struck by an electron beam. The intensity of the glow at any spot on the screen depends on the strength of the beam at that spot. The beam quickly traverses the picture tube returning periodically to each spot on the screen to refresh the glow before the glow dies down. Figure 4.1 shows the scan pattern of the electron beam. Each spot that glows on the screen is called a picture element, or **pixel**.

The electron beam's movement and intensity is determined by signals from a board containing electronic chips and connections. This **graphics adaptor** board resides in the main computer and is activated by signals from the CPU (see Figure 4.2).

The three most popular graphics adaptors for DOS-compatible computers are described below:

Adaptor	Abbreviation	Pixel count (horizontal × vertical)
Color graphics adaptor	CGA	300 × 200 (near obsolete)
Enhanced graphics adaptor	EGA	640 × 350
Video graphics array adaptor	VGA	640 × 480

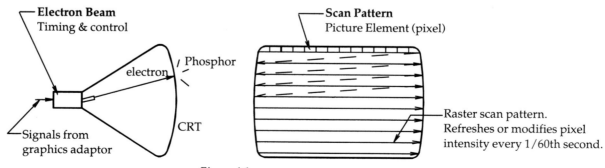

Figure 4.1
LEFT SIDE VIEW AND FRONT VIEW

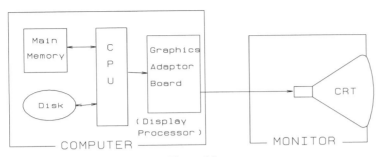

Figure 4.2
GRAPHICS ADAPTOR BOARD

Most PC/ATs contain EGA adaptors (640 × 350 pixels). Since there is a menu and coordinate display on the CRT screen, the actual drawing area on the screen is somewhat less than 640 × 350 pixels. Other boards have higher resolution, but for each increase in pixel count, there is a corresponding increase in cost.

Questions

1. What is a pixel?

2. What is a graphics adaptor?

3. Where is the graphics adaptor located?

4. What is EGA an abbreviation for?

5. What is VGA an abbreviation for?

6. If your computer is not set up to do graphics, what would you need to buy at the minimum to allow it to do graphics?

7. What is the usual pixel count for an EGA computer?

UNITS

The UNITS menu is used to preset measuring units used in the drawing. (Refer to the Reference List on the inside front cover.) Contrast the UNITS and PROPERTIES menus: PROPERTIES presets property features, while UNITS presets values associated with the whole drawing.

■ **Menu Commands**

Units›Increment
Rotation

others

Menu Item   **Comment**

Increment   The smallest movement that the graphics cur-
                     sor makes in the drawing area is from pixel
                     to pixel. If the cursor is to move across the
                     screen from pixel to pixel, it must be turned
                     on, then off, at each pixel in its path, requiring
                     a prodigious amount of signaling.

                     Instead of moving from pixel to pixel, the
                     cursor can be moved by increments. The
                     VersaCAD default increment is ¼ inch, and
                     the cursor remains at a pixel location until the
                     mouse moves the cursor the incremental dis-
                     tance (see Figure 4.3). The cursor then jumps
                     to the next increment, skipping in between
                     pixels. Cursor movement becomes a little
                     jerky, but cursor placement on selected incre-
                     ment points is easier than placement on pixel
                     points.

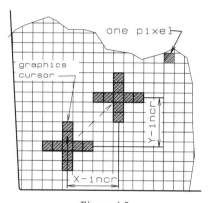

Figure 4.3
BOTTOM LEFT
CORNER OF SCREEN

                     Pixel to pixel movement: The cursor (9 pixels
                     in Figure 4.3) is turned on, then off, as it
                     moves through each pixel location.

                     Increment movement: The cursor is turned
                     on and remains on, even though the mouse
                     moves more than one pixel distance. When
                     the mouse has moved more than one incre-
                     ment distance, the cursor is turned off, then
                     on at the next increment location.

Rotation   The rotation angle is a counterclockwise
                     angle from the positive X-axis direction. The
                     default value for the rotation angle is 90
                     degrees. This angle or a multiple of it defines
                     the R-axis direction.

The [F6] function key allows the user to change a preset or
default property and to change the preset or default value for
Increment and *Rotation*.

❏ EXERCISE: INCREMENT-ROTATION

This exercise allows the user to see the effect of presetting the increment of movement and the rotation angle.

1. Execute Vcad. Select *Drafting*. Select *Add›Line* and pick point 1 anywhere. Select *[F6]›Increment 3* (a 3-inch increment!) and *Quit* back to the LINE menu.

2. Move the cursor to place point 2 but don't pick it. Notice the cursor moves only after the mouse has moved the equivalent of a 3-inch increment.

3. With the point still not picked, select *[F6]›Rotation 30 [enter]› Quit*. Repeatedly select *Rotation* to see the tracking-line movement.

4. End of exercise.

SNAP

Because it is sometimes difficult to stop the cursor precisely at some selected point, VersaCAD contains a feature that allows the user to **snap** the cursor to a preselected point. You access the SNAP menu by pressing the [F2] key. (Like the [F6] key, the [F2] key can be used from any menu.) When you are through using *Snap*, VersaCAD returns you to the menu that was displayed just before you pressed the [F2] key.

Menu Item	Comment
None	No snap. The cursor moves freely.
Increment	Cursor movement is constrained to *Increment* movement.
inTersect	VersaCAD queries "Which intersection?" User picks the desired intersection. Cursor will snap to the user-selected intersection and will remain there until another pick releases it, even though the user might move the mouse around.

■ **Menu Commands**

F2›None
    Increment
    inTersect
    Object

    others

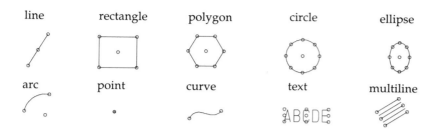

Figure 4.4
HANDLE POINTS

Object	VersaCAD queries "Which object?" User selects uppercase *EQUATION* or lowercase *Equation*, then picks the desired object.
›*EQUATION:*	When the user selects an object and then moves the mouse, the cursor will move, but will remain on the selected object until the next pick.
›*Equation:*	When the user moves the mouse, the cursor moves but is constrained to the "handle" points of the object—predefined points on each VersaCAD object (see Figure 4.4).

Snap to Object

Picture the cursor within an imaginary square. When the user picks an object, the cursor must be close enough to the object so that the square covers some portion of it (see Figure 4.5).

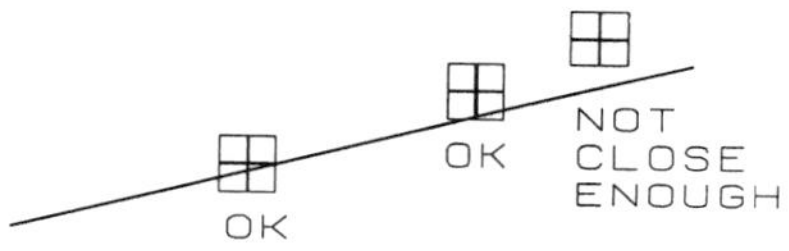

Figure 4.5

Snap to Endpoint

When trying to snap to the endpoint of a line, make sure that the cursor is some distance away from the selected endpoint, not directly over it (see Figure 4.6). This way, you'll know your snap process is correct, since you'll be able to see the cursor jump to the endpoint.

Figure 4.6

❑ EXERCISE: SNAP

1. Execute Vcad. Refer to the previous Window exercise, get $WINDOW again, and redo steps 9, 10, and 11.

2. Precision Placement: Draw the four required lines using [F2]. To snap to the midpoint of a leg of a rectangle, first explode the rectangle into four lines. Keep in mind that although the midpoint of the leg of a rectangle is not a handle, the midpoint of a line is.

3. A stuck cursor: Draw two points, A and B, anywhere. Drawing five connected lines away from the points, let's assume you wish to end the fifth line on point A. At this time select *[F2]›Object›Equation* and make one pick on point A. Before making the second pick on point A, which will record it, you decide to end the line on point B instead. Now you have a problem: The cursor is stuck on point A.

You can free the stuck cursor by pressing the mouse button, but that would still leave the fifth line ending on point A, not B. Try it.

If you select *Detach*, you will erase line 5 instead of freeing the cursor. Try it.

If you select *Erase*, you will erase line 5, but the cursor will still be stuck. Try it.

If you select [escape], you'll free the cursor but erase all five lines. Better not try it.

4. Freeing the cursor: Press [F2]. Make no snap selection, but press the mouse button instead. The cursor can now move without affecting the previously drawn lines.

5. End of exercise.

FATLINES

By selecting *Switches›Fatlines›No*, all objects will be displayed and plotted using width 1 even though some of them have been previously set to different widths. By selecting *Switches›Fatlines›Yes*, objects will be displayed and plotted using the width previously selected for each object.

A *Fatline* display is inconvenient for redrawing and snapping because it takes time to redraw. Also, it's more difficult to snap the cursor to a fatline endpoint because the fatline is wider than the cursor. These problems are avoided by leaving the fatline switch to *No* much of the time. You must remember to select *Switches>Fatlines>Yes* before plotting, however, or all the lines will be plotted as width 1.

CHANGING THE PROPERTIES OF AN EXISTING OBJECT

An existing object's properties can be changed by selecting *Modify>Properties*. All changes made are only proposed changes until you select *Update*. If you quit from *Modify>Properties* without updating, no changes take place.

For example, a red object is red because you have drawn it after selecting *[F6]>Color>Red*. You can now change it to green by selecting *Modify>Properties>Color>Green>Update*. You can also change other existing properties in the same way: select *Modify>Properties*; select the specific property to be changed; then update.

Be sure to recognize the difference between *[F6]>Color>Green*, which will make a *new* object green, and *Modify>Properties> Green>Update*, which will make an *existing* object green.

❏ EXERCISE: CHANGING THE BORDER
(Be sure to do this exercise)

The following exercise allows the border to be drawn faster, while still maintaining wide lines. Currently the border drawing uses Pen 1 and lineWidth 3, so that each object is drawn three times—each time offset by 1/64 inch to increase width. Time can be saved by using Pen 6 (wide pen) and lineWidth 1, so that the plotted line will still be thick but drawn only once.

1. Execute Vcad and select *Drafting*.

2. To change the Pen 1-lineWidth 3 objects in BORDER to Pen 6-lineWidth 1, do the following:

Select *Filer›Get›BORDER. Quit* to the DRAFTING menu.

Select *Switches›Fatlines›Yes›Quit.*

Select *Modify›Properties›Pen›Proposed 6›lineWidth›Proposed 1.*

Note that the forward (>) symbol is now displayed after the *Pen* and *lineWidth* menu items on the screen, indicating that these are proposed changes. Until *Update* is selected, proposed changes do not become actual changes.

3. Select *Update* so that the current object's properties will be updated. After selecting *Update* for one object, the next object in line starts blinking. Select *Update* again so that the next object's properties are also updated, and repeat this until all objects in BORDER are updated. (Updating an already updated object is unnecessary but creates no problem.)

4. *Quit* back to the DRAFTING menu and select *Switches›Fatlines›No›Quit.*

5. Save your new BORDER. Plot it for your reference but do not submit.

Questions

1. What menu selections do you make to preset to Pen 4, Color 2?

2. From the DRAFTING menu, what selections do you make to change an existing red line to Pen 4, Color 2?

3. How many handle points does a line have?

4. How many handle points does a circle have?

5. If *Switches›Fatlines›Yes* is selected, will all objects be plotted fat?

❑ DRAWING: SNAP

Note: These drawings are shown in Figure 4.7.

1. Execute Vcad and select *Drafting*.

2. Separate the drawing area into four parts. Use Pen 6, Width 1 for lettering.

3. Clamp: Use Pen 1, Width 3. Draw the triangle, then explode it as follows:

Select *Modify* and blink the triangle. Notice that the whole triangle blinks.

Select *Explode*. Notice that only one leg now blinks. VersaCAD will now treat the triangle as three separate lines.

Select *Add›Circle*, then use *[F2]›Object* to snap each circle center to a triangle corner. The midpoint of the leg is a handle point. Snap to this handle point for the radius. The circles will be tangent to each other.

4. Wheel: Draw a Width 1, Style 2 circle with marker. Draw polygons, then snap their centers to circle handles. For the square, set the rotation angle to 45 degrees so the square can be drawn with a horizontal base. Orient the other polygons as well.

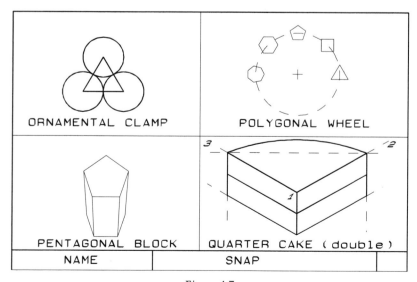

Figure 4.7

5. Block: Use Pen 1, Width 1. Draw two pentagons, then explode the bottom pentagon so the back lines can be erased. Snap the near vertical lines to pentagon corners.

6. Cake: Preset the rotation angle to 30 degrees. Use Pen 6, Width 1. Most snaps will be intersection snaps. Template line directions are some multiple of the rotation angle.

To draw template line 1-2, select *Add›Line›Single*. Pick point 1.

Select *Template›Rotation*. Pick point 2.

Do the same for line 1-3. For point 3, you'll need to select *Rotation* more than once.

Draw the horizontal template line, then the rest of the template lines.

Select *Arc›Three pts* and draw the arc. Finish the rest of the drawing.

7. Before plotting, select *Switches›Templates›No›sKetch*. Also select *Switches›Fatlines›Yes›Quit*. If you forget this, the plot widths will all be Width 1.

8. Plot. Before submitting your plot, examine the effect of using different pens and different widths:

Clamp W-3 P-1

Cake   W-1 P-6

Block W-1 P-1

Wheel W-1 P-1

CHAPTER 5

Modifying

OBJECTIVES

- *To use the computer's power to perform repetitive tasks efficiently.*

- *To use Move, Copy, Rotate, and Scale.*

- *To use VersaCAD to calculate arithmetic expressions.*

- *To introduce the concept of macros.*

- *To introduce Group, which will be explained more fully in a later chapter.*

CHAPTER CONTENTS

Moving an Object

Copying an Object

Exercise: Two Overlaying Objects

Drawing: Copy-Repeat

Rotate, Scale

Drawing: Rotscale

Drawing: More Cop

Exercise: VersaCAD's Expression Evaluator

Macros

Exercise: Macro

Drawing: Groupmac

MOVING AN OBJECT

An object is moved by selecting *Modify›Find*, then moving the desired object. To try this out, execute Vcad and select *Drafting*, then draw a small rectangle in the center of the drawing area. Using this rectangle, select the MOVE menu items described below.

Menu Item	Comment
Original	When *Move* is selected, the object tracks cursor movement. Selecting *Original* will move the object back to its original location.
X-axis	Object is constrained to move in the X-direction only.
Y-axis	Object is constrained to move in the Y-direction only.
Free	X-, Y-, or *Original* constraints are removed.
Handle	Selects an alternate handle for tracking. The user presses *H* a number of times to cycle through the various handle choices. *Note:* The *H* must be pressed twice before the cursor changes from the initial handle.
Swap	Selects an "opposite" handle (for those handles where opposite has meaning).

■ **Menu Commands**

Modify›Move›Handle
X-axis
Y-axis
Free
Original
Swap

COPYING AN OBJECT

When an object is copied, one or many duplicates of the original are produced.

Menu Item	Comment
Handle, X-axis, Y-axis, Free	These four menu items are identical to those for *Move*.
Original	Moves the copy back to its initial location, overlaying the original object.

■ **Menu Commands**

Modify›Copy›Handle
X-axis
Y-axis
Free
Original

Place
Erase
Repeat

Place	Freezes the object so the cursor can move without the object tracking. *X-, Y-* or *Free* will free the cursor.
Erase	A copied object can be recopied numerous times until *Quit* is selected. *Erase* will erase the last copy.
Repeat	Selected when more than one copy is desired. VersaCAD counts the original object as a copy. For example, if you want three copies of an existing rectangle, when VersaCAD asks you how many copies you want, you must respond with "four."
›*One dir*	Copies in any desired single direction.
›*Two dir*	Copies in X-direction and Y-direction.
›*Circular*	Copies from a center point. For example, see Figure 5.1, where *Copy›Repeat›Circular* has been selected with the following specifications:

Incremental Rotation   20˚

Number of copies   2

Object rotation   35˚

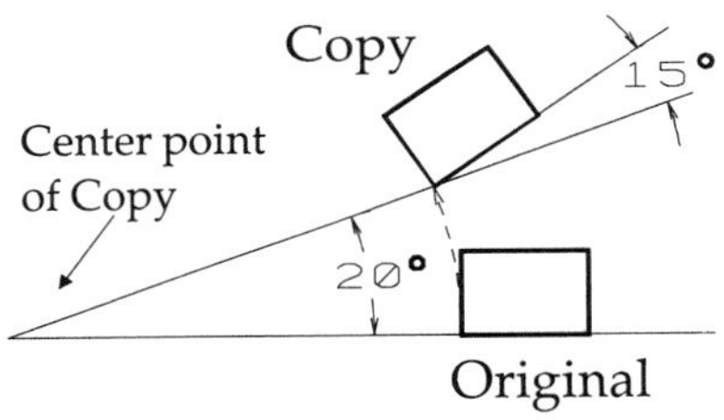

Figure 5.1

❑ EXERCISE: TWO OVERLAYING OBJECTS

This exercise helps to explain the apparent disappearance of an object when a copy is made at the same location.

1. Execute Vcad and select *Drafting*.

2. Draw a rectangle. Make a copy using *Modify›Copy* but don't record (pick) yet.

3. Select *Original*. The object seems to disappear.

4. *Quit* to DRAFTING to suppress blinking. Select *[F5] (Long cursor)*. Place cursor to the left and below the rectangle. Slowly move the cursor up vertically until it overlays a leg of the rectangle (VersaCAD signals tracking overlay by blanking the overlay portion).

5. Now select *[F5] (Short cursor)*, then *Modify›Copy›Original*. Press the mouse button, then *Quit*. The rectangle is again displayed; however, it is actually two rectangles, one overlapping the other.

6. Move the top rectangle using *Modify›Move*. Press the mouse button. VersaCAD displays a rectangle in its moved position by deleting it from its original position, then redrawing it in the moved position. A pixel is "deleted" by making it the same color as the background pixels; however, this process deletes the original rectangle. Select *sKetch* to redisplay the original rectangle.

7. Try the other COPY menu items.

8. End of exercise.

❑ DRAWING: COPY-REPEAT

Note: This drawing is shown in Figure 5.2.

1. Execute Vcad and select *Drafting*.

2. Place a border in the graphics area and fill in the titles.

3. **Framework:** Draw the octagon with thin lines.

Draw the octagon's horizontal diagonal 1-2 using *Snap* for the end points.

Use *Modify›Copy›Repeat›Circular* to draw the other diagonals, using the midpoint of the horizontal diagonal for the center point. The incremental rotation will be 45 degrees and there will be four copies (remember that VersaCAD counts the original as one copy). When VersaCAD asks for the amount of object rotation, just press [enter].

4. **Circles:** Explode the octagon, then draw the bottom circle thick. (Why did the octagon have to be exploded?) Copy this circle so there is one at each corner of the octagon (use *Copy›Repeat›Circular*, of course, unless you like to draw circles).

5. **Rectangles:** Draw the bottom left rectangle thin. Copy it using *Copy›Repeat›One dir*.

6. **Triangles:** Draw the bottom right triangle. Copy with *Copy› Repeat›Two dir*.

7. Plot and submit (remember to use *Switches›Fatlines›Yes)*.

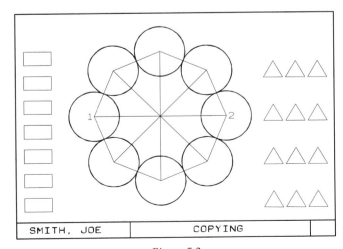

Figure 5.2

ROTATE, SCALE

Menu Item	Comment
Rotate	
›*Pivot*	Selects a pivot point different from the default, which will be shown by a large dot.
›*Handle*	Selects a new handle. Object will track along the pivot-handle line when rotating.
›*Rotate*	Each *R* selection rotates an object by another incremental rotation.
›*Original*	Reverts an object to its original orientation.
›*Zero*	Changes an object's orientation so that the pivot-handle line is an X-axis (zero degree rotation angle).
›*Free*	Frees an object to rotate based on cursor movement.
Scale	
›*Factor*	Shrinks or magnifies an object by the factored amount. For example, if the user enters 0.5, then the object would scale to half size.
›*Handle*	Selects an alternate handle.
›*Unproportional:*	Scales along X-axis or Y-axis only.

■ **Menu Commands**

Modify›Rotate
Scale

❏ DRAWING: ROTSCALE

1. Execute Vcad and select *Drafting*.

2. Make a border with suitable titles.

3. Select *Pen 1*. Explode the border rectangle, explode each of the resulting rectangle legs, and then use handle points to draw one horizontal and three vertical line separators (see Figure 5.3).

4. Draw a rectangle in area 1, then use *Modify›Copy›Repeat› Two dir* to copy the rectangle as shown in the figure.

5. Make the required modifications to the rectangles, based on Figure 5.4.

6. Add the text shown for 1, 2, 3, and 4. For 5, 6, 7, and 8, add your own text, indicating which MODIFY menu items you used.

7. Plot and submit.

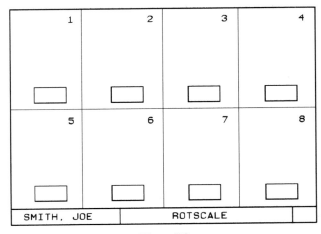

Figure 5.3

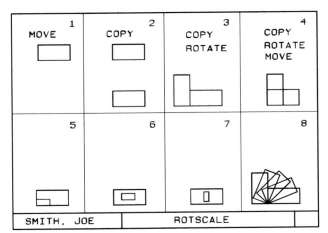

Figure 5.4

❑ DRAWING: MORE COP

Note: This drawing is shown in Figure 5.5.

1. Execute Vcad and select *Drafting.*

2. Use Pen 6, Width 1. Draw border and titles. Draw the outer rectangle of the object.

3. Use *Modify* to make four copies of the outer rectangle directly over the original rectangle. One copy will be used to place the circle centers, then erased.

4. Scale the copies using factors of 0.9, 0.7, 0.5, and 0.4.

5. Center the scaled copies using *Modify›Move.* Select the center of each rectangle as the handle when moving and snap this handle to the center of the outer rectangle.

6. Change the circle rectangle to Style 8 (template). Explode it so the cursor can later be snapped to the midpoint of the rectangle's legs.

7. Draw the top left circle (with marker). (It would be preferable to have thin circle markers, but marker and circle are drawn with the same pen.) *Copy›Repeat* the circle in two directions, snapping to the midpoint of the legs.

8. Erase the unwanted template lines and middle circle.

9. Plot and submit.

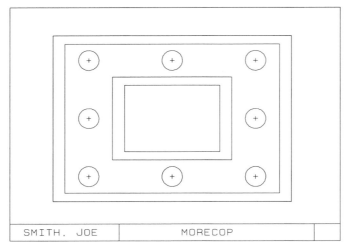

Figure 5.5

❏ EXERCISE: VERSACAD'S EXPRESSION EVALUATOR

1. Execute Vcad and select *Drafting*.

2. Without drawing any object, select *[F6]›Pen 123XYZ*. Note how VersaCAD rejects invalid keyboard entry.

3. Select *Pen 2+3*. Rejected again. The plus (+) character is not a digit.

4. Select *Pen 2+3;* When you place a semicolon after an expression, VersaCAD uses its expression evaluator to evaluate the expression and return the result to VersaCAD, just as though the result itself had been entered at the keyboard.

5. Select *Pen 2*3;* The expression evaluator interprets a star (*) as multiplication and a slash (/) as division. It can even handle parentheses.

6. Select *Pen ((2+3)*2+4)/2;* This is a roundabout way of selecting Pen 7.

7. Select *Text›Width .8*1/2; Height 1/2.* Some people like character width to be smaller than character height. Here the semicolon is used to make the width eight-tenths of the height.

8. Summary: To have a keyboard-entered expression evaluated, terminate the expresson with a semicolon.

9. End of exercise.

MACROS

A macro is a set of instructions that can be executed as though it were a single instruction. To create a macro, press [F9]; notice the word "def" (definition) displayed in the message area. At this point, VersaCAD will store as well as execute all your subsequent instructions until you press [F9] again, which ends the macro creation. To execute the macro later, hold down the [control] key, then press [F10], which can be expressed as [ctrl-F10].

❑ EXERCISE: MACRO

This exercise must be completed in order to finish the next drawing.

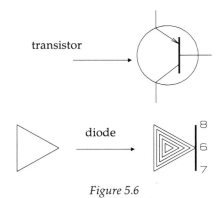

transistor

Figure 5.6

1. Execute Vcad and select *Filer›dRive›I:›Get›$GROUPMA›dRive›B*: (see drawing in Figure 5.6).

2. Transistor: Select *Window›In*.

Place a rectangle around the transistor and pick to make it bigger, then *Quit*.

Finish drawing the lines in the transistor. Use *Snap›Object›Equation* for the outer endpoints. Use *Snap›Object›EQUATION* for the arrowhead endpoint.

Select *Window›Base›Quit*

3. Macro: The triangle on the right is to be filled with smaller triangles by using a number of *Modify›Scales*. From the DRAFT-ING menu, select the following to scale it once; at the same time, create a macro for subsequent scaling:

Begin macro definition by pressing [F9] (notice the word "def" in the display). Select *Modify*, find the triangle, and pick it. Then select *Copy›Original* (the triangle will seem to disappear). Pick the copy and *Quit*.

Select *Scale›Factor*; then to end the macro definition, press [F9] (and note that "def" disappears).

Select *0.2* for the factor.

Select *sKetch*, and the large triangle reappears.

Now to execute the macro and continue scaling, hold down the [control] key then tap [F10] just once. This is touchy. If you hold it down too long, more than one execution will occur. When the macro has finished executing, key in a *0.4* factor.

Do the same by re-executing the macro with [control-F10] for *0.6* and *0.8*.

Again, select *sKetch* to make the large triangle reappear.

4. Extend a line: Preset *lineWidth* to 3. Draw a Y-axis line from point 6 to 7. To stretch the line to point 8, select *Modify›Scale*.

Move the cursor around randomly; you'll notice the line is stretching from the wrong endpoint. Select *Swap* then finish drawing the line. Preset *lineWidth* back to 1. *Quit* to DRAFT-ING.

5. Grouping: Group the diode in Figure 5.6 and move to point 5 as follows:

Select *Group›Build›New›Yes›Fence* in the diode: Every object that is within or even partly within the fence will become part of the group. *Quit* building.

Select *Group›Move*, then use *Snap* to grab the diode at point 6 and move it by snapping to point 5, which is in the middle of the line.

6. Scaling: Shrink the diode to one-fourth its size by selecting *Scale›Stationary point at 5* (see Figure 5.7 for point 5)*›Handle at large triangle center›Factor›0.1.*

7. Save as GROUPMAC (omit dollar sign) for later use. Do not plot.

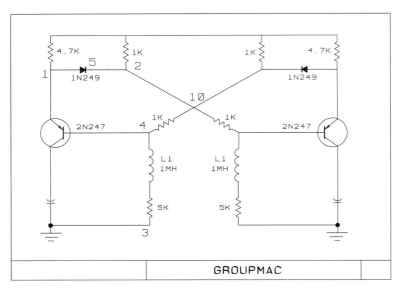

Figure 5.7

❑ DRAWING: GROUPMAC

Note: This drawing is shown in Figure 5.7.

1. Execute Vcad and select *Drafting*. Then select *Filer›Get› GROUPMAC*.

2. Build a group: The resistor at 1 is to be copied to 2, 3, and 4. *Since Modify›Copy* copies only single objects, we must use a different set of commands, because the resistor is a group of objects. To copy this group, select the following:

Select *Group›Build›New›Yes›Fence,* as shown in Figure 5.8, and pick.

Select *Where* to see whether the resistor objects are the only objects in the group, then press the [escape] key. A horizontal line should be removed from the group.

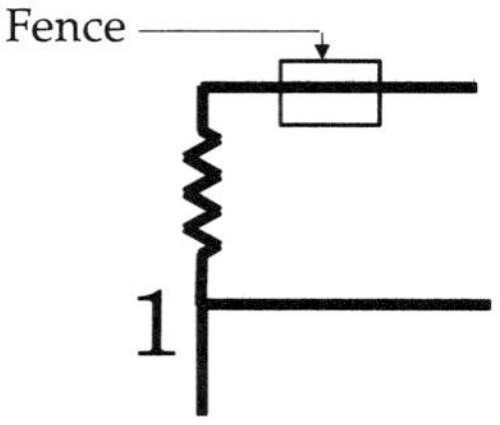

Select *Remove›Fence* in the unwanted line and pick (see Figure 5.9).

Reselect *Where* to verify removal, then *Quit* to the GROUP menu.

3. Group copy: To move the cursor to an existing point on the drawing, snap to it with [F2] (rather than placing it by eye).

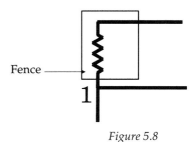

Figure 5.8

Figure 5.9

Copy the point 1 resistor to 2 by selecting *Group›Copy› Single*. Default the new group name by pressing [enter].

Select the handle to be at point 1, the bottom point of the resistor. You'll need to pick a point twice; once to put the cursor on the point and once to select the handle at the cursor location. The "change in direction" is at point 2. Snap to it (two picks).

In a similar manner, select *Single* and copy the resistor to points 3 and 4. The resistor at 4 will have to be rotated after the copy—however, it is not the current group.

To make it the current group, select *Build›New›Yes›Fence* in resistor 4, then *Quit* to the GROUP menu.

Select *Rotate*. Snap the pivot to the resistor bottom. Snap the handle to the resistor top. Snap the cursor to point 10. Resistor 4 is now rotated.

To stretch the top line of the resistor to point 10, *Quit* to DRAFTING and select *Modify›Find* to find the top line, then *Scale* to point 10 using *Snap*.

4. Imaging: Delete the temporary numbering 1, 2, 3, 4, 5, and 10.

Add the necessary text, *Width .8*3/8;* (use the semicolon) *Height 3/8*.

Select *Group›Build›New›Yes›Fence* to fence in the entire object for right-hand imaging, then *Quit*.

Select *Image›Copy›Y-axis*. Snap the image line to point 10. Pick the image.

5. Save as GROUPMAC. Plot and submit.

CHAPTER 6

Constructions

OBJECTIVES

- *To make geometric constructions including tangents, parallels, perpendiculars, chamfers, and fillets.*

- *To trim, extend, and break objects.*

CHAPTER CONTENTS

FILLETS

VersaCAD classifies as fillets both fillets and rounds. The user selects two objects for the fillet. When two joined lines are filleted, the choices that result are numerous (consider the results in Figure 6.1). The menu items that follow are selected to achieve the desired end result.

Menu Item	Comment
Radius	The radius of a fillet is a preset value, initially the same as the default increment value. Select *Radius* to change the preset value.
Circle	Selected if the whole circle, rather than the arc fillet, is desired.
SMALL	The smaller fillet (shown uppercase, initially) is the default option.
Large	Select *Large* to create the larger fillet. *SMALL* becomes lowercase *Small*.
TRIM	*TRIM* (uppercase) is the default option. If *TRIM* is selected *Automatic* and *Manual* menu items disappear, and the *TRIM* menu item becomes lowercase. In the lowercase *Trim* mode, the fillet is drawn and no trimming occurs. To reinstate trimming, the user selects *Trim*. Then *TRIM, Automatic,* and *Manual* reappear as menu items.
AUTOMATIC	*AUTOMATIC* trimming is the default option. The user picks the two lines to be filleted, and trimming occurs automatically.

■ Menu Commands

Construct›Fillet›
　　　　Radius
　　　　Circle
　　　　SMALL
　　　　Large
　　　　TRIM
　　　　AUTOMATIC
　　　　Manual
　　　　Erase

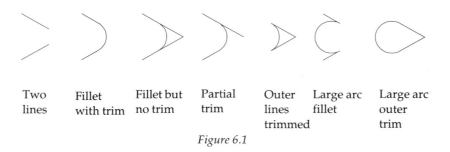

Two lines	Fillet with trim	Fillet but no trim	Partial trim	Outer lines trimmed	Large arc fillet	Large arc outer trim

Figure 6.1

Manual	If partial trimming is desired, select *Manual*, then pick the two lines. Portions of each will blink in turn.
›Yes	Trims the blinking portion and causes the next portion to blink.
›Next	Blinking portion is not trimmed. The next position blinks.
›Quit	Accepts the fillet with its current trimming.
Erase	Erases the fillet and reverts back to the original lines.

TANGENTS

Menu Item	Comment
Free	Arc to point tangent: The user selects an arc, circle, or ellipse object and a line tangent to the object will track to the cursor. The user selects *Next* to have the other tangent track to the cursor. The user picks to record the cursor. (See Figure 6.2.)
Tangent	Arc to arc tangent: The user selects two arcs and a tangent is drawn. If the wrong tangent is displayed the user repeatedly selects *Next* until the correct tangent is displayed. The user then picks to record the tangent. (See Figure 6.2.)

■ **Menu Commands**

Construct›Tangent›
      Free
      Tangent
      Parallel
      Normal

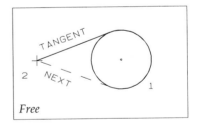

Free

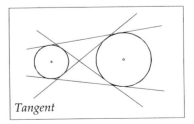

Tangent

Figure 6.2

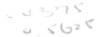

| *Parallel* | Tangent parallel to a baseline: When the user selects an arc and a baseline, a tracking line is displayed tangent to the arc and parallel to the baseline. *Next* is selected if the wrong tangent is displayed (see Figure 6.3). |

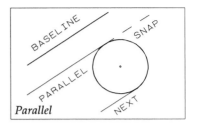
Parallel

| *Normal* | Tangent normal to a baseline: Same as parallel but tracking tangent is normal to (perpendicular to) the baseline (see Figure 6.3). |

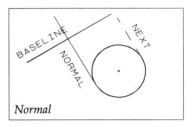
Normal

Figure 6.3

❑ DRAWING: TANGENTS-FILLETS

Note: This drawing is shown in Figure 6.4.

1. Execute Vcad and select *Drafting.* Select *Units›Units.* Repeatedly press the [spacebar] to cycle through the unit choices. Select *Inches Decimal,* then press [enter]. Select *Grid› Xspacing 2›Xdiv 1›Yspacing 2›Ydiv 1* and *Quit* to the DRAFTING menu.

2. Switches: To see the grid turn off and on, select *Switches› Grid›No.* Then select *Switches›Grid›Yes›Quit.*

3. Press *[F6]›Width 3›Quit.*

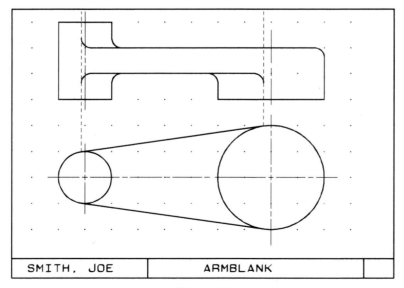

| SMITH, JOE | ARMBLANK |

Figure 6.4

Draw circles using grid points to determine size. Draw tangents.

Draw top view excluding fillets and centerlines. Make the tangent lines in the top view too short. They will be lengthened when the fillets are drawn.

4. Fillets: Use *[F2]›Object*. Draw two vertical template lines from the front-view endpoints of the tangent line in preparation for extending the top view of the tangent lines.

Draw all fillets with a 0.75-inch radius. Normally, the template lines would be removed, but leave them in for this drawing to demonstrate your understanding of fillet locations.

5. Centerlines: Suggested lengths for centerline measurements are long dash (1 inch), gap ($\frac{1}{16}$ inch), short dash ($\frac{1}{8}$ inch). Style 5 lines are inadequate as centerlines when markers are used because the short dashes fall in the wrong place and the gaps and dashes come out the wrong length. Many CAD drafters use a thin, Style 1, line. For this drawing, the centerlines are few and the grid can be an aid in drawing the centerline.

Select *[F6]›Increment›0.2* and change the grid to *Xspacing 2›Xdiv 1›Yspacing 2›Ydiv 1.*

Use the grid points to help draw each centerline as a number of Style 1 lines. Use a long dash of about 2 grid units, a gap of 1 increment unit, and a short dash of 2 increment units. You will need to vary some long dash lengths to fit the marker locations.

6. Merge in a border. Outlines should be thick, centerlines thin.

7. Plot (the grid will not be plotted) and submit.

CHANGING UNITS

The coordinate display at the bottom right of the monitor screen locates the cursor by displaying its coordinates. By selecting *Units›Units* then pressing the [spacebar] or [backspace] key, the user can cycle through the choices of units that can be used to display these coordinates. Your choice is recorded by pressing the [enter] key. The following list shows examples of what the coordinate display might be for a selection:

Unit Choice	Coordinate Display
inches	in [24", 14.1/2"]
inches as feet	in [2'-0",1'-2.1/2"]
inches decimal	in [24.000, 14.5000]
feet	ft [24'-0", 14-6']
feet as inches	ft [288', 174']
feet decimal	ft [24.000, 14.500]
miles	mi [24.000, 14.500]
millimeters	mm [24.000, 14.500]
meters	m [24.000, 14.500]
kilometers	km [24.000, 14.500]

user defined

The user can define a unit not on the list by defining it as a factor of a unit already on the list. When you select *user defined*, you key in the information requested by VersaCAD. For example: Select *Units›Units* then use the [spacebar] to cycle through unit choices until "user defined" is displayed. Key in your responses to the requested information as follows:

Units›Units   drawing units: *User defined*   eq. dwg. units: *feet*
              eq. abbreviation: *yd*   eq. dwg. factor: *3*

Any equivalent abbreviation (such as *yd*) must contain no more than two letters. The resulting coordinate display would appear as: yd[24.000, 14.500].

Units›Units is usually selected before objects are created. If you select a unit and draw an object, you can no longer change the unit. If you select *Inches* and then later select *Units›Units*, VersaCAD will display only the *Inches, Inches as feet,* and *Inches decimal* choices.

CHANGING BASES

The base is the length of the graphics area; the default value is 30 units, with the origin (0, 0) at the bottom-left of the graphics area (see Figure 6.5). Select *Units›Base* to change the base. *Left* and *Bottom* are usually kept at 0, but not always. For example, select a base of 10:

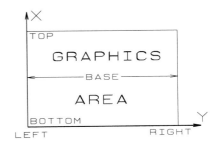

Figure 6.5

Units›Base›   Left: *0* (X = 0)   Bottom: *0* (Y = 0)
Right: *10* (X = 10)   Top: Y-value calculated by VersaCAD

For a special application, you can also define a base of 10 as:

Units›Base›   Left: *-5*   Bottom: *12*
Right: *+5*   Top: Calculated

ARROW AND MARKER SIZES

Arrow and marker sizes are set up by default to be of reasonable size on the screen and on the plot compared to the default base of 30. However, when you change the base size, arrow and marker size do not change accordingly. Say you changed the base size to 10—arrows and markers would then be three times as large as they were, compared with the new base size. Therefore, when you change base size significantly, you will need to change arrow and marker size as well—which you do by selecting *Output›Units›Factor*.

The menu selections for *Output›Units* are enumerated below for reference but without elaboration since our current interest is only with *Output›Units›Factor*. *Device* refers to whichever device is being used for output, usually a plotter. The *world* is the area used to locate the objects to be drawn. *World coordinates* are the coordinates shown in the coordinate display at the lower right of the monitor screen.

Menu Item	Comment
Units	Output device units: inches/millimeters.
Factor	User can press [enter] for default plot specifications or can respond with desired inches on paper and inches on screen.
Text	Scale type: world/device (device refers to the plotter).
Dimension	Scale type: world/device: Slash length: 1/8". Object offset: 1/16". Outside length: 1/4". Outside chord: 5/32".
lineStyle	Scale type: world device: Pattern length: 1". Doubling the pattern length doubles the length of a dash in a dashed line on the plot.
lineWidth	Scale type: world/device: Increment: 1/64". Shift: 0.6250.
Arrow	Scale type: world/device: Arrow type: open/closed. Length: 1/8". Doubling the arrow length doubles the length of arrows on the plot. Incl. angle: 20 degrees.
Marker	Scale type: world/device: Size: 1/16".

❑ EXERCISE: ARROW-MARKER SIZE

1. Execute Vcad and select *Drafting*.

2. Select a base of 10 units with *Units›Base*. Draw a line with an arrow and a circle with a marker. Notice the arrow and marker appear too large.

3. Select *Output›Units›Factor›[escape]*. The current factor is displayed.

4. Let's assume an arrowhead is ⅛-inch long on a plot. This size may make the arrowhead too small or too large on the screen, depending on the factor, which is a ratio of (plot length)/(length represented on the screen). If the current factor is 0.3333, then 0.3333 inch on the plot displays as a 1 inch length on the screen. To reduce the arrowhead to one-third its current screen size without affecting its size on the plot do the following:

Select *Output›Units›Factor›[enter]* (we are not yet using plot specs).

Inches on paper: *0.3333* (this is the current factor).

Inches on screen: *1/3* (this is the amount of screen reduction required).

5. End of exercise.

❑ DRAWING: MORE TANGENTS AND FILLETS

Note: This drawing is shown in Figure 6.6.

1. Execute Vcad and select *Drafting*.

2. Select a base of 10 (left: 0, right: 10). Use a 1-inch grid with five divisions between grid points. (Do not draw the border now, but leave room for it.)

3. Draw the views shown in the figure. Since the views are not complete, complete them using the suggestions below:

Outlines:	If no markers: Width 1, Broad pen 6.
	With markers: Width 2, Narrow pen 1 (you may prefer Width 3).
Hidden lines:	Width 1, Narrow pen 1.
Centerlines:	Width 1, Narrow pen 1.

4. Before adding centerlines, note that the markers are too large on the screen. Change marker size with *Output›Units›Factor.*

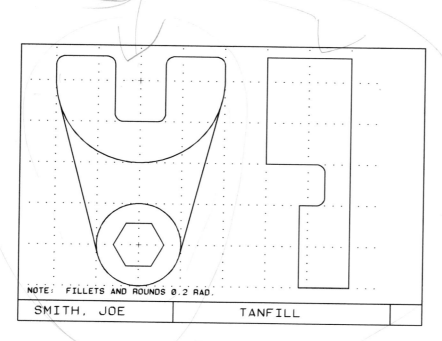

Figure 6.6

scale
1/1. or 10/10

5. Add centerlines to both views, keeping the views separate (don't join the views with a single centerline). Be sure you have drawn in the runouts with fillets in the view on the right. For reference, examine the runouts and fillets on the drawing in Figure 6.4.

6. Border: The previously stored border with its 30-inch base will be too large when merged into our 10-inch base drawing. If you have not used the *Group* menu item yet, there are no members in the current group. *Merge* in your too-large border and key in *Yes* when asked if the merged drawing should be placed in the current group. You can then reduce the size of the merged border as follows:

Select *Group›Scale*. Place the stationary point at the lower left corner of the border. The *Handle* point can be placed anywhere since the use of *Factor* next will cancel its meaning. Select a *Factor* of *10/30;*—use the semicolon (current drawing base is 10; the border's base was 30).

You may then have to use *Group›Move* to arrange the reduced border in a more convenient location.

7. Plot and submit.

TRIMMING AND EXTENDING

When two objects need to be trimmed or extended so they meet as desired, the user selects two objects and then chooses which portions of each object to extend or trim. Note that the menu item *Construct›Extend* is used for both extending and trimming; there is no *Construct›Trim*. Referring to the objects in Figures 6.7 through 6.13, read through the exercise, then do it at the computer station.

■ **Menu Commands**
Construct›Extend›   *Automatic*   *Manual*

❏ EXERCISE: TRIM-EXTEND

1. Execute *Vcad›Drafting* and select *Filer›dRive:›I:›Get $TRIM›dRive›B:*

2. Select *Construct›Extend.*

3. *AUTOMATIC* is the default. Pick lines 1 and 2, and they will join. Select *Erase*, then *Manual*. Pick 1 and 2 again. For this case, *Automatic* and *Manual* produce the same result.

Select *Automatic*. Pick line 3 and the B portion of line 4. Line 3 will extend to line 4 and the A part of line 4 will be trimmed. Erase. Try again, selecting A this time. B will be trimmed. Erase. Try again. This time select A or B before you pick line 3.

Select *Manual*. Pick line 3 and line 4. Line 3 will extend to line 4. Line 4 will blink. Pick A or B. The selected part will be trimmed. Erase. Try again.

4. You may wish to trim one or more of lines C, D, E, or F. Using *Erase*, try both *Automatic* and *Manual* a number of times. Notice that in *AUTOMATIC* mode, if you pick one end of a line the other end is trimmed. In *Manual* mode, if you pick one end of a blinking line, it is trimmed and the other end remains.

5. Many choices are involved in trimming or extending an arc-line combination. Arc GH could be trimmed or extended to resulting arc G, H, GH, JGH, or GHK. Line XY could be trimmed or extended to resulting line X, Y, Z, or XYZ. Select *Next* to toggle through choices. Either record the choice or select *Quit*, then work on the other object.

6. Remove the top-left corner of the rectangle by first exploding the rectangle, then trimming. This trimming is the same as the trimming done in step 5.

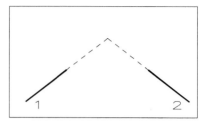

Figure 6.7

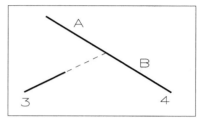

Figure 6.8

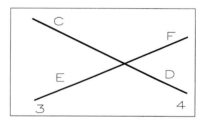

Figure 6.9

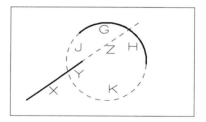

Figure 6.10

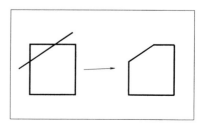

Figure 6.11

7. Assume you wish to keep only the top-left slice of the circle. Use *Construct›Break›Fence*, then remove some of the lower part of the circle. *Quit.* Select *Construct›Extend* for trimming the arc and line that remain.

8. To extend line M, do not use *Construct›Extend* since there is only one object. Instead select *Modify›Find›Scale.* You may have to swap ends.

9. End of exercise.

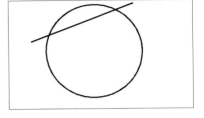

Figure 6.12

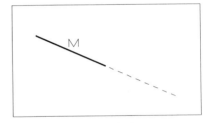

Figure 6.13

❏ DRAWING: TRIM-EXTEND

Note: This drawing is shown in Figure 6.14.

1. Execute Vcad and select *Drafting*.

2. Select *Units›Base›0›10›0*. Then select *Units›Grid›X & Y space 1/2, Div 1*. Finally, select *[F6]›Incr 1/4›Pen 6›Width 1.* Do not draw the border yet, but leave room for it.

3. Draw five circles, properly located, in the view on the right of the drawing in Figure 6.14. Some of these circles will be trimmed later. Draw the tangent lines.

4. Circle trimming: Trim the bottom circle.

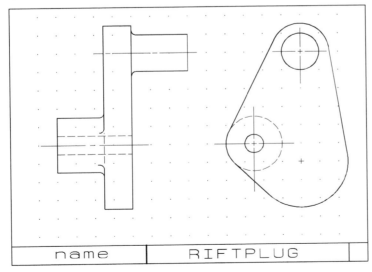

Figure 6.14

Select *Construct›Break›Fence*. Fence in a small, unwanted piece of the circle. Circle-line combinations cannot be trimmed without first breaking the circle.

Quit, then select *Construct›Extend* and trim the circle to the desired arc. Trim the top circle in a similar manner.

5. Dashed arc: Remove the portion of the circle that is to be dashed.

Select *Break›Fence,* then *Extend›Trim.*

Add the dashed arc by first changing to Style 2, then select *Add›Arc›Centr/2 pts.* Snap to the center of the dashed arc.

6. Left view: Draw the view on the left in Figure 6.14 (excluding centerlines) using ¼-inch fillets. Runouts should be projected from the tangent ends in the right view, using temporary solid lines. (If template lines are used, the subsequent fillet may become a template fillet).

7. Merge in your too-large border and reduce it by 10/30.

8. Centerlines: Select *[F6]›Increment›1/16"›Pen›1.* Since the left view does not contain markers, you could use Style 5 for the centerlines. For the right view, window in on the centerline areas and draw centerlines using an approximately 1-inch long dash, a 1/16-inch gap, and a 1/8-inch short dash. Use *[F6]›Increment 1/16* as an aid. Make use of *Modify›Copy›Repeat›Circular* for these center lines.

9. Select *Window›Base.* Outlines should be thick. Hidden and centerlines should be thin.

10. Plot and submit.

NORMALS

A normal is a line perpendicular to another line called the baseline. The user selects the baseline, then the two endpoints of the normal.

Menu Item	**Comment**
Distance	After selecting the baseline and endpoint 1, the user can select *Distance*, then key in a number to change the location of endpoint 1 of the normal. For example, after picking point 1, the user selects *Distance 5* and picks point 2 (see Figure 6.15).
Rotation	The user can select *Rotation*, then key in *50* to change the 90 degree angle of the normal with the baseline. The normal is then no longer a "normal." The angle is measured counterclockwise from the baseline toward point 2 (see Figure 6.16).
Original	This option is for those who change their minds and want the earlier point 1 or the earlier 90 degrees back.
Snap	Snaps the second endpoint of the normal to the baseline.

■ **Menu Commands**

Construct›Normal›
          Arrow
          Template
          Marker
          Distance
          Rotation
          ORIGINAL
          Snap

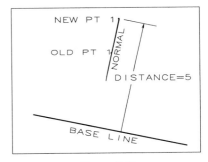

Figure 6.15

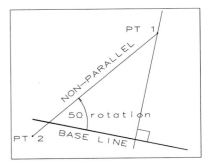

Figure 6.16

PARALLELS

Parallel menu items are identical to normal menu items (see Figures 6.17 and 6.18).

❏ DRAWING: NORMAL-PARALLEL

Note: This drawing is shown in Figure 6.19.

1. Execute Vcad and select *Drafting*.

2. Use a base of 40. Use *Inches, decimal* units.

3. Begin by drawing the hexagon, then the centerlines to the two circles (these centerlines will be erased later). CONSTRUCT menu items will be needed for this drawing, including *Construct›Parallel*.

4. Draw the object. Do not dimension. Break the 1.75 R circles before filleting. They can be trimmed during filleting. Add a border.

5. Plot and submit.

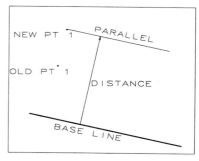

Figure 6.17

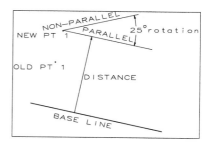

Figure 6.18

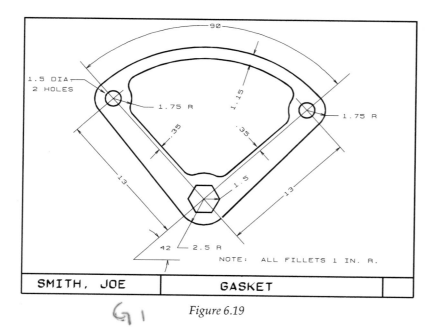

Figure 6.19

Trimming Note: VersaCAD can trim a line and an arc, but cannot trim two arcs. You can work around this deficiency by drawing a construction line, then trimming each arc to the construction line. Draw the first endpoint of the line using *[F2]›inTersect*. The second endpoint can be placed anywhere. Erase the construction line after trimming (see Figure 6.20).

Occasionally, when the user is pointing at a 2-arc intersection, VersaCAD inexplicably bombs out of the program, reddening the screen background and returning the user to the main menu. You then have no choice but to reboot by pressing the [control-alt-delete] keys simultaneously, re-entering VersaCAD, and then trimming the 2-arc intersection by the less accurate method of windowing in and drawing the construction line by eye, without a snap.

Figure 6.20

CHAPTER 7

Dimensioning

OBJECTIVES

- *To draw linear and angular dimensions.*
- *To input data by methods other than mouse picking.*
- *To input absolute, relative, and polar coordinates.*
- *To change origins.*
- *To use levels.*

CHAPTER CONTENTS

Linear Dimensioning

Drawing: Linear Dimension

Angular Dimensioning

Drawing: Angle Dimension

Input Modes

Drawing: Input

Levels

Dimension Settings

Radial Dimensioning

Drawing: Radial

Block Text

Drawing: Block Text

LINEAR DIMENSIONING

Dimensioning requires a superabundance of information input. The user must select from the following menu items:

Menu Item	Comment

Dimensioning Method

Single   Default selection.

Baseline   See Figure 7.1.

Chain   See Figure 7.1. Also, select *Height* for a different height in the chain.

Two-Point Selection Method

Object   For selection of the two points, the cursor need only be near an object endpoint for the dimension to snap to that endpoint.

Two pts   Used when at least one point is not an endpoint. [F2] (snap) is required for point placement.

Pick the Two Points

Press the mouse button and select two points.

Select Dimension-Line Features

Initially a dimension-extension line set will display oriented along the X-axis.

X-axis   Select one of these menu items if change in
Y-axis   orientation is desired (see Figure 7.2).
True angle

Extension   User repeatedly selects *Extension* to retain one or both of the extension lines (see Figure 7.3).

■ Menu Commands
Dimension›Linear

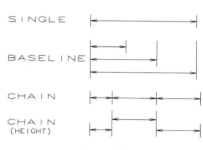

Figure 7.1

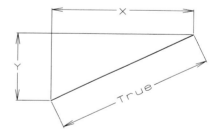

Figure 7.2

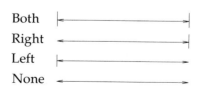

Figure 7.3

Markers	Markers for dimensioning are at the ends of the dimension lines (see Figure 7.4). They are not center markers. User repeatedly selects *Marker* to toggle through the variety of markers available.

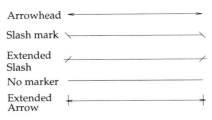

Figure 7.4

Pick the Dimension Depth

Select Text Options

Locate, orient, and format the text associated with a dimension.

X-axis *Y-axis* *True*	Orients the text to the given axis (see Figure 7.5).

Figure 7.5

Rotate	Rotates the text to the R-axis (see Figure 7.6).
Break	Breaks the dimension line so text can be placed within it (see Figure 7.7).
Outside	Places the arrows outside the extension (see Figure 7.8)

Figure 7.6

Lock	Text remains within limits of the dimension line. User reselects *Lock* to place text anywhere on the drawing.
Center	Centers the text within the dimension line.
Precision	Selects the number of digits to the right of the decimal point.
Decimal	Selects between decimal text (1.25) or fraction text (1¼).

Figure 7.7

Feet	Displays text in feet and inches.
Inches	Displays text in inches only.
Edit	Allows text editing. The user can key in a dimension text different from the VersaCAD-calculated one.
Undo	Undoes the last dimension. Pressing [escape] eliminates *all* dimensions in a baseline dimension.

Figure 7.8

❑ DRAWING: LINEAR DIMENSION

Note: This drawing is shown in Figure 7.9.

1. Execute Vcad and select *Filer>dRive>I:>Get>$DIMEN>dRive>*
B:

2. Merge in a border. Add titles. Preset *Width 1, Color 5, Pen
5, Text height and width 0.3* for the dimensions.

3. Chain: Select *Dimension>Linear>Chain* to enter the top four
dimensions. Select *Decimal,* then *Precision 2.* Use the [spacebar]
to change the precision number. For the third dimension,
change *HEIGHT* to *Height* so the dimension line can be raised.
Use the long cursor to line up the height of the fourth dimension.

4. Baseline: Select *Baseline* and enter the bottom three dimensions.

5. Extension: For the 3.00 dimension, repeatedly select *Extension* until just one extension is displayed (the correct one).

6. Precision: For the Z dimension (bottom right), select *Y-axis*
and make the *Precision 0.* Use the [spacebar] or the [backspace]
key to change the default precision number.

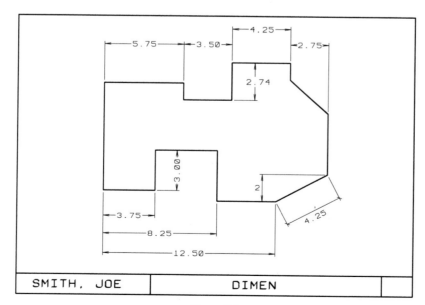

Figure 7.9

7. Marker: For the slanted 4.25 dimension, select *True* and repeatedly press *Marker* to change from arrowhead to slant line.

8. Edit: The 2.74 dimension requires an *Edit*. You want 2.74 but VersaCAD has calculated 2.75. (You should not have to use *Edit* for any other dimension if you're dimensioning correctly.)

9. Save your drawing as DIMEN (without the dollar sign). Plot and submit.

ANGULAR DIMENSIONING

The text options for angular dimensioning are the same as the text options for linear dimensioning. Please note that since the keyboard does not have a degree symbol, the decimal is used to indicate degrees. For example:

24	same as 24 degrees
14.5′ 15″	same as 14 degrees 5 minutes 15 seconds
12.2′	same as 12 degrees 2 minutes
12.2	same as 12.2 degrees (decimal notation)

An angular dimension requires that the angle be defined by selecting a vertex, and legs 1 and 2. It also requires that the dimension line, the extension line, and the text be located.

Menu Item	Comment
Single, Baseline, Chain	These menu items have the same effect as in linear dimensioning.
Three pts	User defines a vertex and two points for legs. If any of the three points are to be on an object, the user must use snap for accuracy.
Object	User selects the two legs of the desired angle; their intersection will be the angle's vertex. Each leg will have an extension line; the extension line begins at the leg endpoint that was nearest the cursor when the user selected the leg. Therefore, the user can select

■ **Menu Commands**

Dimension›Angular

either side of the midpoint of the leg for the beginning of the extension line.

Extension   User repeatedly selects *Extension* to cycle through the visibility choices for extension lines (see Figure 7.10).

Direction   Either the smaller or larger angle might be dimensioned. VersaCAD measures angles counterclockwise by default from leg 1 to leg 2. User selects *Direction* to measure clockwise (see Figure 7.10).

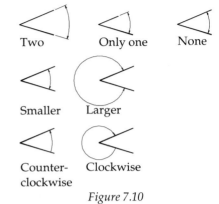

Two   Only one   None

Smaller   Larger

Counter-   Clockwise
clockwise

Figure 7.10

❑ DRAWING: ANGLE DIMENSION

Note: This drawing is shown in Figure 7.11.

1. Execute Vcad and select *Filer›dRive›I:›Get›$ANGLES› dRive›B:* Outlines are purposely plotted with a light-colored pen (Pen 5, Color 5) so that the proper use of extension lines can be checked. Pen 1, Color 1, Width 1, and 17/64-inch text should be used for dimensioning.

~ 3/8 ˝

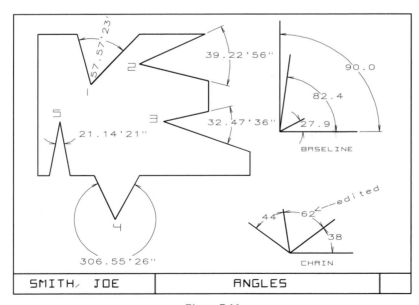

Figure 7.11

2. Angularly dimension the given objects using the exact dimensions shown in Figure 7.11. *Object* rather than *Three pts* is usually easier to use; with *Three pts*, each point must be snapped but with *Object*, snapping isn't needed.

Recognize the differences between angles 1 through 5:

Angle 1 is an internal dimension.

Angle 2 is an external dimension.

Angle 3 is part internal and part external.

Angle 4 is a larger dimension.

Angle 5 is an outside dimension. *Outside* is selected after the second point is picked.

Note: VersaCAD often gives the error message "Object defined is too small. Press RETURN to continue." This is a valid error message when the text is too large to place within the extension lines. Reposition the dimension or shrink the text size. Sometimes this error message occurs even before you try to place the dimension, an obvious bug in the VersaCAD program. Simply press [enter] and select your two points a second time. If the error message persists, try selecting the second point on the other side of the midpoint of the second leg of the angle. Still no success? Then select *Three pts* rather than *Object*. You'll have to snap to the vertex and legs.

3. Just prior to plotting, select *Switches›Fatlines›Yes›sKetch› Quit.*

4. Plot and submit.

INPUT MODES

The INPUT MODE menu, displayed by pressing the [F1] key, allows the user to alternate between mouse input and keyboard coordinate input to select points in a drawing. With mouse input, you move the cursor and click a mouse button to pick a point. With coordinate input, you key in two coordinates. In this way, you draw on the screen. (If you use the mouse during coordinate input mode, the cursor moves [uselessly] and clicking the mouse button has no effect.) No track-

■ Menu Commands
[F1]›Mouse
Absolute
Relative
Polar

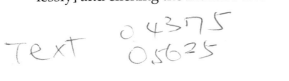

ing occurs. Three types of coordinates are used within VersaCAD; absolute, relative, and polar coordinates.

Absolute and Relative Coordinates

The absolute coordinates of a point are its coordinates as measured from the origin of the drawing. The default origin of a drawing is the lower left corner of the graphics area. In Figure 7.12, the absolute coordinates of point 1 are (5, 8) and the absolute coordinates of point 2 are (15, 17).

The relative coordinates of a point are the coordinates of that point relative to the previous point. In the same figure, the relative coordinates of point 2 are (10, 9) and the relative coordinates of point 1 with respect to point 2 are (-10, -9).

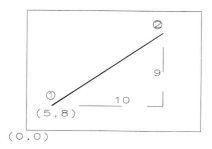

Figure 7.12

Polar Coordinates

The *polar angle* of point 4 with respect to point 3 is defined as an angle with vertex at point 3, with the positive X-axis as the first leg, and line 3-4 as the second leg.

In Figure 7.13, the *polar coordinates* of point 4 are (30, 7). The first coordinate is the polar angle, and the second coordinate is the *polar distance* (the distance from the previous point).

Point 4 has many polar coordinates with respect to point 3, depending on how the polar angle is measured. Two alternate coordinates for point 4 are (-330, 7) and (210, -7). You should be able to determine at least two more: (__ ,__) and (__ ,__).

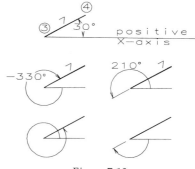

Figure 7.13

The Menu Select Key

When a user has pressed the [F1] key and selected *Absolute, Relative,* or *Polar* input, VersaCAD treats subsequent keyboard entry as the coordinate input. If a line is being drawn and an arrow is desired, the user must signal VersaCAD that the next entry will be a menu selection, rather than a coordinate input.

The [menu select] key is a back apostrophe (') located at the top-left corner of the keyboard. The user presses [menu select], then *A* to make an arrow selection. The user can then key in the coordinates of the second point of the arrowed line. Other menu selections are made in a similar manner. *Caution:* The key repeats if held down more than three seconds. Two back apostrophes with an *A* ("*A*) will not produce an arrow.

The Input-Mode Toggle [alt-F1]

Suppose you are drawing lines using relative input mode. If a momentary switch from relative input to mouse input is required for the next endpoint, the [alt-F1] input toggle can be used (hold down the [alt] key, then press the [F1] key). After you select the next endpoint with the mouse, you can toggle back to relative input by again selecting [alt-F1].

Shifting Origins

It's sometimes convenient to shift the origin from the lower left corner of the drawing area to some other location. Select *[F3]›Origin*, move the cursor, and pick a new origin. An alternate method is to select *[F1]›Absolute›[F3]›Origin*, and then key in the coordinates of the new origin.

Select *[F3]›Origin›Clear* to change the origin back to the bottom left corner of the drawing area. For example, referring to the drawings in Figures 7.14 and 7.15, suppose you have previously selected (2, 5) as a new origin but you now wish to select another new origin, at (8, 9). Either of the following will do the job:

[F1]›Absolute›[F3]›Origin›6,4

[F3]›Origin›Clear›[F1]›Absolute›[F3]›Origin›8,9

Selecting the latter without clearing the origin would be a blunder. The new origin would end up at (10, 14).

■ **Menu Commands**

*[F3]›Origin›Clear
Shift*

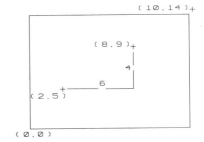

Figure 7.14
COORDINATES FOR
DEFAULT ORIGIN

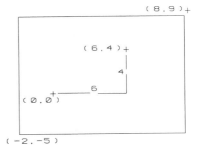

Figure 7.15
COORDINATES FOR
ORIGIN AT (2, 5)

❑ DRAWING: INPUT

Note: This drawing is shown in Figure 7.16.

1. Execute Vcad and select *Drafting*.

2. Make border and titles.

3. Absolute: Select *[F1]›Absolute›[F3]›Origin* and shift to the new origin at (4, 14). Not on the screen, but in pencil on this page, replace the (4, 14) with its current absolute coordinates (0, 0). Going clockwise, pencil in the absolute coordinates of the rest of the points in the absolute figure. The first, second, and third coordinates would be (0, 0), (0, 5) and (10, 5).

Draw the absolute figure by selecting *Add›Line* and keying in absolute coordinates.

4. Relative: Select *[F3]›Origin›Clear*. Whoops! VersaCAD assumes the C is part of a number being entered (see screen). Press [backspace], then the menu select [‘] key, and then *Clear*.

Move the cursor to the bottom left of the graphics area. Read the displayed coordinates, verifying that the origin has changed to bottom left. Use *[F1]›Absolute›[F3]›Origin* to shift the origin to (4, 5).

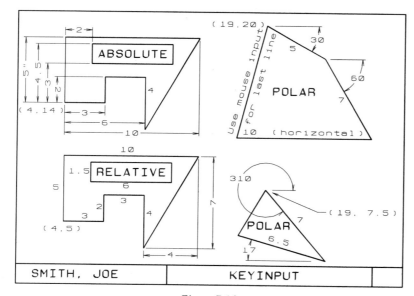

Figure 7.16

Pencil in the relative coordinates going clockwise. The first three are (0, 0), (0, 5) and (10, 0).

To draw the figure, select the first point as absolute (0, 0), then the rest as relative coordinates.

5. Polar: In a similar manner, draw the polar figures. Enter the first point as absolute (0, 0), then the rest—except for the last point—as polar coordinates.

6. Linear dimensioning: For the absolute object, select *Dimension›Linear›Baseline.* Change color so the extension lines can be seen. Draw all linear dimensions.

7. Angular dimensioning: For the 310-degree angle, select *Angular›Three pts* instead of *Angular›Object.* Snap twice to the vertex, then select *[F2]›Object›EQUATION* to snap to the existing leg. VersaCAD will measure the angle from the +X direction. The 30- and 60-degree angles dimension similarly, but *Direction* will also be needed.

The 17-degree angle requires more effort. It is not measured from the +X direction. Before dimensioning it, add a construction line of any convenient length from the 17-degree vertex in the +X direction. Then select *Dimension›Angular›Single›Three pts.* Snap to the vertex with *[F2]›Object›Equation.* Snap the first leg point to the arrowhead location on the 6.5 line using *[F2]›Object›EQUATION.* Then use *[F2]›Object›EQUATION* again on the construction line in the +X direction, moving the cursor along this construction line. Select the second point on the *extension* of the construction line to the left of, but near to, the vertex. The third point is obvious. Finally, erase the construction line.

8. Complete the drawing. Make outlines thick, dimensions thin.

9. Plot and submit.

LEVELS

A level is an alternate graphics display that can replace or overlay the current graphics area. As an example of the use of levels, consider the drawing plans for a house that requires a floor plan together with foundation, electrical, plumbing, and water supply layouts. The CAD drafter can draw each layout separately on a different level (a different screen display). Then by selectively turning levels on or off, the drafter can display or plot, in overlay fashion, any combination of these layouts.

Various Screen Areas

Figure 7.17 illustrates VersaCAD's various screen areas. With 250 graphics levels available, if you draw a line on level 1 and a circle on level 2, then at any given time you can display either or both in the graphics area.

Drawing on Different Levels

The default drawing level is level 1—you've been drawing on level 1 for some time now. To draw on a different level, select *[F6]›Level* and key in a level number. Only one level can be drawn on at a time.

■ Menu Commands
Switches›Levels›
Yes
No
Up
Down
Jump
[backspace]
[spacebar]
Quit

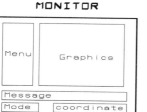

Figure 7.17

```
Level #:  15
12345678901234567890123456789012345678901234567890
YY..Y.YY...YYYYYYYYYYYYYYYYYYYYYYYYYYYYYYYYYYYYYYYY
```

Figure 7.18

Turning Off Levels

Initially, all 250 levels are turned on, but there are no objects in any of them. To choose which levels to turn off, select *Switches› Levels*; VersaCAD will display 50 level numbers (as many as the screen can hold at one time). To display a different 50, use the menu option *Up* or *Down* or *Jump›Number*. See Figure 7.18, which shows VersaCAD awaiting a user decision on level 15. Levels 3, 4, 6, 9, 10, and 11 are turned off. Use the [spacebar] or a menu item to select a level number, with *Yes* or *No* for on or off. A dot (.) is shown for *No*, because it makes the line easier to read.

Displaying All Levels

To display all levels (even the ones that are turned off), select *Switches›All levels›Yes*. Selecting *Switches›All levels›No* displays turned-on levels only.

Changing the Level of an Existing Object

Use *Modify›Find›Properties›Level›Number›Update*. If there are numerous objects to change, group them, then use *Group› Properties›Level*.

DIMENSION SETTINGS

When a user begins dimensioning, default settings for marker type, center, lock, precision, and other options already exist. The setup menu allows you to preset these defaults to other values.

Menu Item	Comment
Default	Returns all dimensioning options to their default settings.
Tolerance	Presets a tolerance for linear dimensions (see Figure 7.19).
›Type	Cycles through *None, Limit, Plus-minus* when [spacebar] is pressed.
›Limits	Requests lower and upper preset limits for a linear dimension. Angular dimensions are not toleranced.
Lock, Break, Outside, Center, Markers, Units, Precision	After one of these settings is selected, pressing the [spacebar] causes VersaCAD to cycle through the value choices.

> ■ **Menu Commands**
>
> *Dimension›Setup›*
> *Default*
> *Tolerance*
> *Lock*
> *Break*
> *Outside*
> *Center*
> *Markers*
> *Units*
> *Precision*

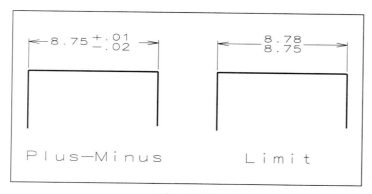

Figure 7.19
TOLERANCE

RADIAL DIMENSIONING

A radial dimension is used to dimension circles or arcs. The radius or diameter dimension line can be placed inside or outside the object to be dimensioned.

Menu Item	Comment
Radius	Uses a radius for the dimension.
Diameter	Uses a diameter for the dimension (circles only, no arcs).
Outside	Toggles the origin of the extension line from the center to the outside of the object.
Rotate, Free	Rotates the dimension line by an amount equal to the preset rotation angle. *Free* releases the dimension line from its R-axis direction.
Precision, deCimal, feeT, Inches, Edit, Undo	Selecting any of these menu items creates the same effect as with linear and angular dimensioning.

■ Menu Commands

Dimension›Radial›
  Radius
  Diameter

  Outside

  Rotate
  Free

  Precision

  deCimal
  feeT
  Inches

  Edit
  Undo

❏ DRAWING: RADIAL

Note: This drawing is shown in Figure 7.20.

1. Execute Vcad and select *Drafting*.

2. Setup: Select *Units›Inches, decimal.* Choose a base of 10 units. You will be making judicious use of *Switches›Levels* and *Switches›All Levels.* Place the border on level 2 by using *[F6]›Level›2.*

3. Draw: Switching to level 1 for the objects, complete the drawing (Pen 6) without including dimensions.

To draw the 37-degree line, select *[F6]›Rotation›180-37;› Quit.* Draw a 37-degree line anywhere. It will be erased later. Select *Construct›Tangent›Parallel* to draw the desired 37-degree line, which will eventually be trimmed.

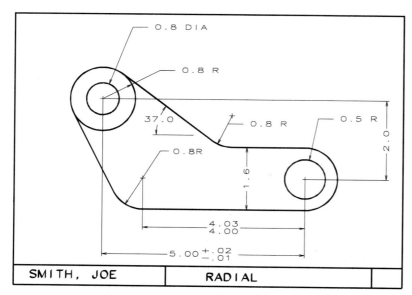

Figure 7.20

To draw the arc connecting the 37-degree line, the arc center
will have to be determined using some construction lines,
which will later be erased. Select *Construct›Parallel›Distance* to
draw a line parallel to the 37-degree line and 0.8 units above
it. Also draw a parallel above the horizontal line connecting
the desired arc. The intersection of these two construction lines
is the desired arc center. Draw it as a circle, then do some
trimming.

4. Dimension: Select *[F6]›Level 3›Color 5›Width 1*, then dimension the object.

When dimensioning the lower left radius, the dimension text
cannot be placed without overlapping object lines or dimension lines. *Dimension›Radial* is not always effective. For this
dimension, use *Add›Text* and *Add›Line*.

5. Plot with dimensions: Submit. Experiment a little with
Switches›Levels and *Switches›All Levels* to get a feel for their
usage.

BLOCK TEXT

When *Add›Text* is selected and text is keyed in, the user has the option of pressing the [enter] key then locating one line of text, or selecting *Block* (paragraph) mode and entering a number of lines of text. The [control] key is held down while another key is pressed.

Menu Item	Comment
[ctrl-I] (Up) *[ctrl-K] (Down)* *[ctrl-J] (Left)* *[ctrl-L] (Right)*	*Block* mode is automatically selected and the current line of text is moved in the direction indicated. Up-down movement is determined by the preset *[F6]›Text›Row* value. Right-left movement is determined by the preset *[F6]›Text›Column* value.
[ctrl-R] (Rotate)	Rotates the text by the preset rotation amount.
[ctrl-B] (Block)	Selects *Block* mode and writes *BLOCK* as uppercase, or selects *Single line* mode and writes *Block* as lowercase.
[ctrl-E] (Erase)	Erases the current line. Makes the previous line (if any) the current line.
Rotate *Block* *Erase*	After selecting [enter] for the current line, the user can still rotate, erase, or select *Block* mode. These selections do not require the [control] key.

■ Menu Commands

Add›Text›[control]
> *I (Up)*
> *K (Down)*
> *J (Left)*
> *L (Right)*
>
> *R (Rotate)*
>
> *B (Block)*
>
> *E (Erase)*

Row Spacing

Spacing between lines of text, called row spacing, is achieved by selecting *[F6]›Text* and then selecting *lineWidth* and *Height*. Typically, row spacing for a paragraph of text is twice the size of the height of the chosen font; column size (tab space) is one-and-a-half times the height; for example, *[F6]›Text›Width 3/8›Height 3/8›Font 1›Column:1.5*3/8;›Row:2*3/8;*

If the user does not notice that the row spacing is incorrect until the second line is being typed, then the following method can be used to change this row spacing:

1. Select [ctrl-I] (up) to superimpose the second line over the first.

2. Select *[F6]›Text* and change *Row* to the desired spacing.

3. Press [F6] and quit, then select [ctrl-K] (down) and continue entering text.

❏ DRAWING: BLOCK TEXT

Note: This drawing is shown in Figure 7.21.

1. Execute Vcad and select *Drafting*.

2. Use a base of 37, select *Units›Units›Inches decimal*, then draw a border.

3. Preset text width and height to 0.4.

Add the table's first line of text (the column heads LOC, X, and Y) using the default Single-line mode.

Add the rest of the table's lines of text using *Block* mode.

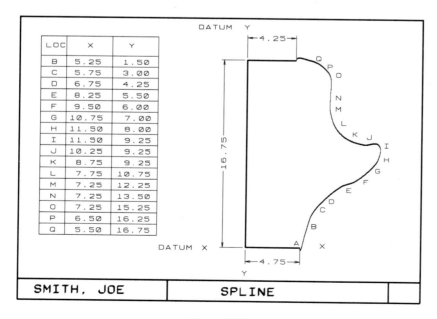

Figure 7.21

Box in the table and draw the inner lines.

4. Draw the straight line portions of the given object.

Change the origin to the lower left of the template object.

Select *[F1]›Absolute.* Select *Add›Line* and enter point A as (4.75, 0).

5. Enter the absolute coordinates in the table up to K.

6. Delete the lines from A through K and try a different method. Select *Add›Bezier›Spline.* Begin the spline at (4.75, 0) and enter all the points. The curve will not begin to draw until the fourth point is entered. The final short curve is drawn when you select *Quit.*

7. Finish the drawing and place the letters A through Q on the object by eye.

8. Plot and submit.

CHAPTER 8

Groups

OBJECTIVE

- *To modify a group of objects as though the group were a single object.*

CHAPTER CONTENTS

GROUPNAME

A groupname is one of the properties of an object; each newly created object is given the default groupname NEW. If you prefer a different name for the default, select [F6] or *Properties* to change it. If you want to change an existing object's group-name, use *Modify›Properties›Groupname›Update.*

Groupnames are part of an object's record—which, you will recall, is a set of data containing an object's geometry and properties. The following are examples of records:

Record Number	Object Name	Geometry	Properties
1	line	X1,Y1, X2, Y2	width, style, color, ... groupname, ...
2	circle	X1, Y1, radius	width, style, color, ... groupname, ...

THE CURRENT GROUP

The current group is a set of objects selected by the user with *Group›Build.* The groupname of an object doesn't change when you select it to be in the current group. Hence, two objects in the current group may have different groupnames. VersaCAD records the objects in the current group by record number (not groupname) in a "current group list."

If you select *Group›Build›New,* a new current group is begun and the old current group no longer exists. If you want to be able to reform the old current group at a later time, you must first make all objects in that group have the same groupname (select *Group›Properties›Groupname*) before you begin a new current group. For instance, if you wish to reform the objects in a group with groupname CHAIRS, select *Group›Build›New› Properties›Groupname›CHAIRS* to make these objects the cur-rent group.

Quitting to the DRAFTING menu doesn't destroy the current group. At any later time you can select *GROUP* to resume manipulating the current group. After quitting to the DRAFT-ING menu, if any new objects are added to the drawing with *Add*, they do not become members of the current group: The only way to become a member of the current group is through *Group›Build*.

GROUP MENU ITEMS

A group is first built, then manipulated or inventoried.

Menu Item	**Comment**
Build	Add objects to the current group.

Modify

Move, Copy Rotate, Scale Image, Explode Properties Delete Undelete	Each of these modifies the current group as though it were a single object. The result is that each object in the group is modified.

Inventory

List	Lists all the groupnames that have been used so far as well as the number of objects that have that groupname, for example: NEW (26) CHAIRS (12)
Where	Identifies the objects in the current group by blinking them.
Number	Selects a start number, to be used later when the current group is copied. (Refer to Moving or Copying the Current Group later in this chapter.)
View	Makes an isometric top view, left view, or right view from an orthographic view. (Covered in detail in the following chapter on pictorials.)

■ Menu Commands

Group›Build

> *Move*
> *Copy*
> *Rotate*
> *Scale*
> *Image*

> *Explode*
> *Properties*
> *Delete*
> *Undelete*

> *List*
> *Where*
> *Number*
> *View*

> *mOre . . .*
> *Undo*
> *Xchange*

mOre . . .	There are too many menu items to fit in the menu area. Selecting *mOre* displays the rest of the GROUP menu items (*Undo* and *Xchange*).
Undo	Undoes the last group *Move, Rotate,* or *Scale.*
Xchange	Exchanges a current symbol with one selected by the user.

BUILDING A GROUP

To modify a group, the user must first build the group.

Menu Item	Comment
New	Blanks the current group list. The current group will then have no members.
Add	Selects objects to be added to the current group. This is the default option for *Group› Build.*
Remove	Selects objects to be *removed* from the current group list, using the same selection method as in *Add.*
Inverse	Builds a new current group containing all the objects that are not now in the current group.
Subset	Builds a subset of the objects in the current group by using *Build›Add* and ignoring all objects outside the current group. For example, if *Fence* is selected, only the objects within the fence and within the current group will become members of the subset. The subset becomes the new current group, replacing the existing current group. However, if *Inverse* had previously been selected, the subset is removed from the existing current group instead of replacing it.
Choose	Uses the cursor to select objects to add to the current group. The user picks an object to

```
■ Menu Commands

Group›Build›New
         Add
         Remove
         Inverse
         Subset
         Choose
         Properties
         Fence
         Objects
```

	make it blink, then selects *Confirm* to add the object to the current group.
Properties	Selects a property. All objects in the drawing with the selected property will be added to the current group.
Fence	Draws a rectangle. All objects that are completely or partly in the rectangle will be added to the current group.
Objects	The *Add* menu will be displayed. The user selects an object by name and all objects in the drawing with this name will be added to the current group. For example, if the user selects *Circle*, all circles will be added to the current group.

MOVING OR COPYING THE CURRENT GROUP

Moving

When the current group is moved with *Group›Move*, each object in the group is moved and the geometric information within each object's record is updated.

Copying

When the current group is copied, new objects are added to the drawing but not to the current group. Selecting *Group›Build* is the only way to add objects to the current group.

Objects in the current group may have different groupnames, but if one copy of the current group is created, all of the copied objects will have the same groupname. If two copies of the current group are created, all of the objects within copy 2 will have the same groupname, not necessarily the same as the common groupname for the objects in copy 1.

When the user selects *Group›Copy* to make two copies, VersaCAD responds with: "New group name (. . . for auto increment)?" The user's response will determine the common groupnames for objects in each copy.

User Keys In	Copy 1	Copy 2	
[enter]	NEW	NEW	New objects are assigned the preset groupname, in this case, NEW.
SAM	SAM	SAM	All new objects have the groupname SAM.
SAM...	SAM1	SAM2	Copy 1 and Copy 2 objects get different groupnames. (Note the three dots in the last entry.)
SAM...	SAM23	SAM24	This result would occur if the user had previously selected *Group>Number 23*.

❑ DRAWING: GROUP CIRCULAR COPY

Note: This drawing is shown in Figure 8.1. You will be drawing half a gear tooth for the right gear, then image-copying it to form a full tooth. This tooth is then copied eighteen times to

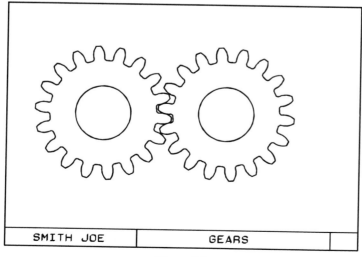

Figure 8.1

form the complete right gear. The gear is then image-copied to form the left gear. Easy! The biggest task is forming the half tooth.

1. Execute Vcad and select *Drafting*.

2. Use a 30-inch base and decimal inches as units (leave the border for later). Choose a center for the right gear. Draw five circles and a vertical line (see Figure 8.2).

3. **Half tooth:** Preset color to red (see Figure 8.3), then find point 1 by drawing the 1.25R circle on the right. Then use point 1 to draw a second 1.25R circle. Delete the right 1.25R circle. Preset color to green (see Figure 8.4), then find points 4 and 5, the ends of the half tooth, as follows:

Draw a 0.44R circle.

Draw a line from C to 3 and image-copy it to create line C-2. Use *Modify›Scale* to extend C-2 to 4. Draw a line from 4 to 6, the top end of the tooth arc. Draw a line from 5 to 7, the bottom end of the tooth arc.

Draw the fillet at 7.

4. **Full tooth:** Group the half tooth. To image it about line of symmetry, C-4, select *Group›Image›Copy›Snap to line C-4›Rotate*. Delete all unnecessary construction lines. Save what you have so far, then continue (see Figure 8.5).

5. **Right gear:** Group the whole tooth. Make it all one color. Then select *Group›Copy›Circular* eighteen times for the whole tooth, using *360/18;* as the incremental rotation.

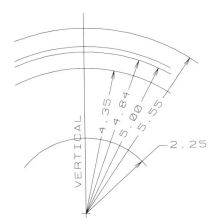

Figure 8.2

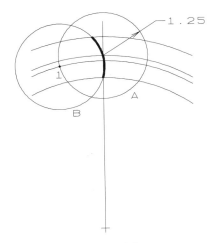

Figure 8.3

6. Left gear: Group the whole right gear. Draw an X-line to the left from point C. To form the left gear, use a Y-image line through the point where the X-line intersects the tooth with *Group›Image›Copy*. When imaging, select *LEFT* as the new groupname.

7. Mesh the gears: At this point, the teeth of the gears overlap instead of meshing. Use *Group›Build›New›Yes›Properties› groupName›LEFT* to make the left gear the current group. Image (without copying) this LEFT group about an X-image line through the center of the left gear. The gears now mesh.

8. Border: Select *Group›Build›New›Yes›Inverse* to group both gears. Center the gears, then merge in a border.

9. Plot and submit.

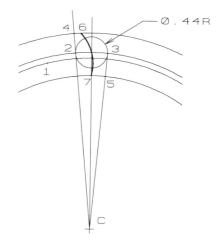

Figure 8.4

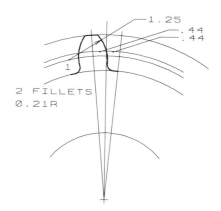

Figure 8.5

CHAPTER 9

Pictorials

OBJECTIVES

- *To use two different methods and their combination to make isometric drawings.*

- *To make an oblique drawing.*

- *To use ellipses.*

CHAPTER CONTENTS

PICTORIALS

A pictorial is a drawing that emphasizes the three-dimensional features of an object. In contrast to a multiview drawing, which describes the size (dimensions) of an object, a pictorial drawing describes its shape (visualization).

The three common types of pictorials are isometrics, obliques, and perspectives. VersaCAD contains menu items that allow the user to draw isometrics efficiently. There are no special menu items for obliques or perspectives; however, the author has developed a technique that allows isometric menu items to be adapted to obliques (which will be discussed later).

An alternate and promising approach to drawing isometric and perspective pictorials is to use VersaCAD's *Modeling* command rather than its *Drafting* command from the main menu. *Modeling* is described in Chapters 14 and 15. The *Drafting* approach is covered in this chapter.

Polar Isometrics

One method for drawing isometrics is to use polar coordinates for much of the drawing. For example, you can use the mouse to define point A on the drawing in Figure 9.1. Then select [F1]›*Polar* for the other points:

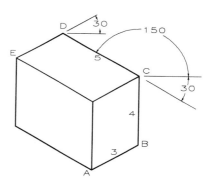

Figure 9.1

Point	Angle	Distance
B	30	3
C	90	4
D	-30	-5 (150, 5 could also be used)
E	30	-3 (210, 3 could also be used)

Continue the process in a similar manner. It's probably easier to make the polar angles +30 or -30 rather than 150 and 210.

INQUIRE

Select *Inquire* from the DRAFTING menu to have VersaCAD calculate and display an object's geometry and properties. After reading the comments below, draw a couple of lines and a circle, then try out the INQUIRE menu items.

```
┌─────────────────────────────┐
│  ■  Menu Commands           │
├─────────────────────────────┤
│      Inquire›Objects        │
│            dRive            │
│            Drawing          │
│            Measure          │
│            Show all         │
└─────────────────────────────┘
```

Menu Item	Comment
Objects	User selects an object with *Find*. The geometry of the object (endpoint, coordinates, length, angle . . .) or its properties (color, style . . .) can be displayed by choosing appropriate menu items.
dRive	Same as the menu item *Filer›dRive*. Used, if needed, before selecting *Drawing*.
Drawing	User enters a drawing name or simply presses [enter] for the workfile. The level numbers and pen numbers used in the drawing are displayed.
Measure	
›Measure	User selects point 1. Point 2 is the current cursor location. Geometric data about line 1-2 is displayed and updated as the user moves the cursor.
›Change	Displays relative coordinates of point 2.
›Length	Displays length of line 1-2.
›Rotation	Displays angle of rotation of line 1-2.
›First point	Displays the coordinates of point 1 and displays all geometry associated with previously selected points 1 and 2.
Show all	Displays all geometry associated with previously selected points 1 and 2.

❏ DRAWING: ISO-1

Note: This drawing in shown in Figure 9.2.

1. Execute Vcad and select *Drafting*.

2. Draw the given isometric as follows: Since the object will easily fit in the graphics area with a base of 10, select base 10. Draw a red isometric box into which the object just fits. Use a combination of *[F1]›Mouse* and *[F1]›Polar* to draw.

3. Since it's now obvious that base 10 is too large, move the box near the graphics area origin so that it won't move off the screen when you change bases. Select *Units›Base›5*. You'll find this base is a little too small. Finally select base 6, then use *Group* to centrally place the red box, allowing for a border to be drawn in later. Use *Inquire* to check the length of one edge of the box. This will verify that base changes do not affect the measurements.

4. Change to Color white, Width 1, Broad pen 6. Draw the object using *[F1]›Mouse* and *Polar*; occasionally use *Modify›Copy*. Dimensions are not required. Leave in the red box as a reminder of the technique.

5. Draw a border and title the drawing ISO-1.

6. Plot and submit.

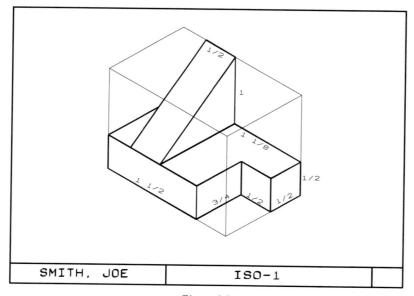

Figure 9.2

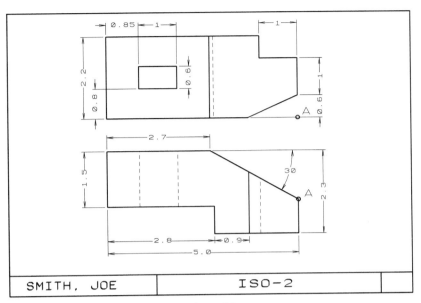

SMITH, JOE   ISO-2

Figure 9.3

❑ DRAWING: ISO-2

Note: The dimensions for this drawing are shown in Figure 9.3.

1. Execute Vcad and select *Drafting.*

2. Draw a red isometric outline box to help center your drawing. Then draw Figure 9.3 as an isometric. Do not draw the top and front views that are shown. Just use the information in these views to draw the isometric. Do not dimension the isometric.

3. Plot and submit as ISO-2.

Comment: Angles are not in true size in an isometric. In an empty corner of the screen, draw a front-view construction triangle to help locate the point-A distance (see Figure 9.4). Transfer this distance to the isometric, then delete the construction triangle.

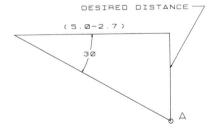

Figure 9.4

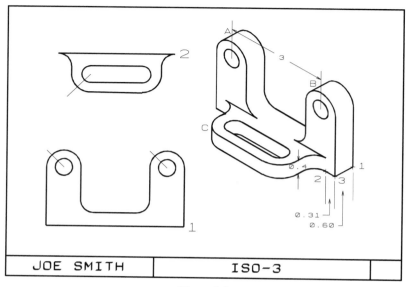

| JOE SMITH | ISO-3 | |

Figure 9.5

❑ DRAWING: ISO-3 ISOMETRICS

Note: Information for this drawing is shown in Figure 9.5.

An isometric drawing may be created from a multiview drawing by grouping a view (the front view, for example), then transforming this view into one or more isometric planes (the left plane, for example) (see Figure 9.6). The ISO-3 drawing in Figure 9.5 consists mainly of two left planes transformed and copied from the partial front view, and two top planes transformed and copied from the partial top view. Do the following:

1. Execute Vcad and select *Filer›dRive›I:›Get›$ISO3›dRive›B:*

2. Draw a red isometric box that will just fit around that portion of the object that is described in the front view. Place it conveniently. Some measurements will have to be extracted from the front view by using *Inquire* and by using temporary dimensioning.

3. Two points will be critical points when making the isometric. Using *Add›pOint›Marker*, draw points 1, 2, and 3 on the isometric box.

4. Front: Group the front view, then select *Group›View›Copy› Left.* Use the front-view point 1 as the handle and the isometric

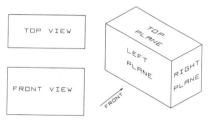

Figure 9.6

point 1 as the new location. The front view will be transformed to a left plane and copied to the isometric. Copy an identical left plane at point 3. *Note:* Text, dimensions, and ellipses will not be transformed using *Group›View*.

5. Top: Group the top view. Then select *Group›View›Copy›Top*. Use the top-view point 2 as the handle and create two top planes in a similar manner. Use *[F1]›Polar* for the point 0.4 units above point 2.

6. Tangents: Circles become ellipses in an isometric. Unfortunately, VersaCAD currently can draw a tangent only to arcs and circles and not to ellipses. The 45-degree lines in the top and front views that emanate from the arc centers will aid in drawing tangent lines. Draw three tangent lines (A, B, and C), using *[F2]›inTersect*. Delete the temporary 45-degree lines.

7. Cleanup: *Delete, Break, Trim,* and *Extend* to complete the isometric. Since isometric dimensioning is not a feature of VersaCAD, use *Add* instead of *Dimension* when you want to dimension. Try one dimension. Dimension the centers with a 3-unit dimension as shown in Figure 9.5.

8. Plot and save the drawing as GROUPISO for your future reference, but do not submit it.

9. Group the isometric and select *Filer›Save›Group›ISO-3*. Then select *Filer›Get›ISO-3* to retrieve it without the orthographic views. Make a border.

10. Plot and submit as ISO-3.

❏ DRAWING: ISO-4 ISOMETRICS

Note: This drawing is shown in Figure 9.7.

1. Execute Vcad and select *Drafting*.

2. Draw the necessary parts of the top and front views. Use *Group›View* to make an isometric drawing (no dimensioning).

3. Delete top and front views and move the isometric to the bottom-left corner in preparation for changing the base for better sizing.

4. Select *Units›Base* and size the isometric (make it fill the screen, leaving room for a border).

5. Add a border.

6. Plot and submit as ISO-4.

Comment: VersaCAD sometimes has difficulty trimming ellipses. You can work around this VersaCAD bug by windowing in on the intersection of the two ellipses; drawing a temporary line in a convenient direction through the ellipse intersections by using *[F2]›inTersect*; trimming to this temporary line; and then erasing the line.

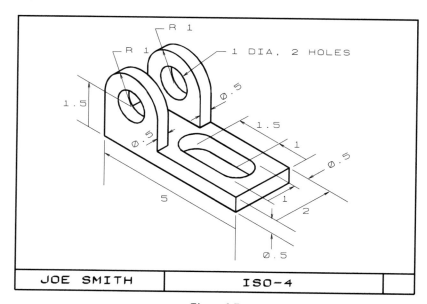

Figure 9.7

OBLIQUES

Isometric drawings contain top, left, and right planes. Oblique drawings contain top, front, and right planes. (*Note:* see Figure 9.8.)

A *right plane* of a 60-degree-to-the-right oblique drawing can be obtained from the right-side view of the orthographic drawing by using *Group›View›Copy›Right›Angle 60.*

A *front plane* can be obtained directly from the front-view orthographic, without the use of *View,* by using *Group›Copy.*

A *top plane* can be obtained from the top-view orthographic in two steps:

1. Select *Group›View›Copy›Right›Angle (90-60);* You are using an angle that is the complement of the previous right plane angle. Place this new view temporarily out of the way.

2. Use *Group›Build›New* to make this new view the current group. Rotate the new view clockwise as follows:

   Select *Rotate* and snap to a pivot point. Change to *[F1]›Polar.*

   Select *Angle 0, any distance* (for example, 10) to define the +X-axis direction.

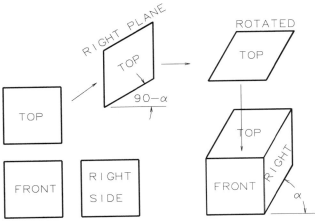

Figure 9.8

Select *Angle -30* (minus 30)›*distance 10* to rotate clockwise.

Place this new view in the oblique's top-view location.

❑ DRAWING: OBLIQUES

Using the ideas just presented, create the drawing shown in Figure 9.9. Plot and submit.

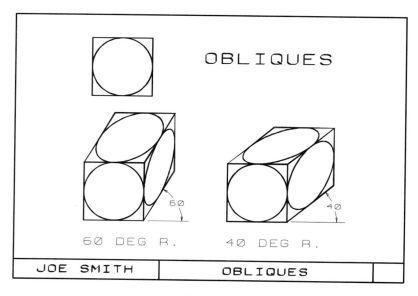

Figure 9.9

❑ DRAWING: ELLIP-1

Note: The drawing for this exercise can be found in Figure 9.10. The drawing is almost symmetrical about a Y-axis. You can draw the left side, image-copy it and correct the nonsymmetrical parts.

1. Execute Vcad and select *Drafting.*

2. Draw an X-axis temporary ellipse in the top-right corner of the screen. You will copy it, then erase it later. Draw a vertical axis (see Figure 9.10). Copy the ellipse four times; rotate the fourth copy 90 degrees.

3. On the temporary ellipse in the top-right corner, draw a major axis and trim off the top half of the ellipse. Then image-copy the bottom of the ellipse about the major axis (two half-ellipses) and change the top half to Style 2, dashed.

4. In the main drawing, trim the solid lines that will become dashed lines. Then copy the dashed half-ellipse to the trimmed locations, trimming the half-ellipse when necessary.

5. Finish the drawing. Make solid lines Width 3 and dashed lines Width 1.

6. Plot and submit.

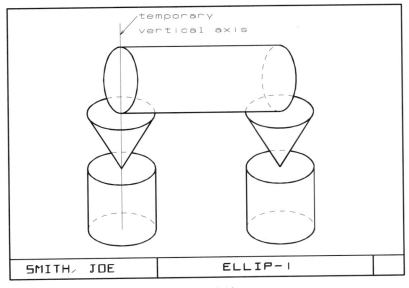

Figure 9.10

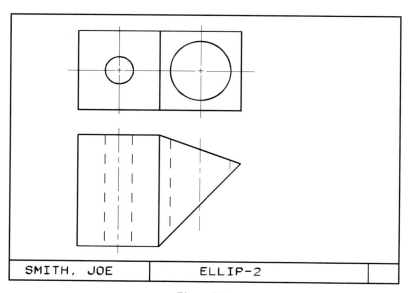

Figure 9.11

❑ DRAWING: ELLIP-2

Note: Refer to Figure 9.11 for this drawing.

An ellipse can be created by defining its center and its axes endpoints (see Figure 9.12). It can also be created by constructing a rectangle, exploding the rectangle, then using the midpoints of the legs of the rectangle to define the endpoints of the axes of the ellipse (see Figure 9.13). The construction rectangle is then deleted. The rectangle method will be used in this drawing.

1. Execute Vcad and select *Filer›dRive›I:›Get›$ELLIP-2› dRive›B*:

2. Draw the right side view.

3. Plot and submit.

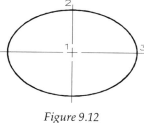

Figure 9.12
AXES ONLY

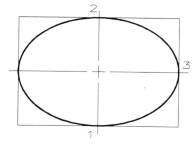

Figure 9.13
CENTR/AXES

CHAPTER 10

Hatching

OBJECTIVE

- *To learn hatching methods*

CHAPTER CONTENTS

Hatching

Drawing: Hatch-1

Drawing: Assembly

Hatch Fills

HATCHING

Hatch is selected when the user wants to crosshatch an area. The user must select the boundaries of the area and the hatch pattern.

After reading the menu items below, practice using *Hatch* by drawing a few areas, then hatching them. Select *Filer›dRive›I:› Get›$HATCH›dRive›B:* and follow the instructions.

Menu Item	Comment
New	Clears any previously picked boundary.
Pick	Picks (or unpicks) objects that define the boundary of the hatch area. As with *Modify*, an object blinks when *Pick* is selected. However, the blinking object is not included in the boundary until the user selects *All* or *Partial*.
›Next	If the wrong object is blinking, the user moves the cursor and picks another object, or selects the backward [<] or forward [>] key to blink the next object. If an object is picked but an overlaying or nearby object blinks instead, then the user selects *Next*. If jerky cursor movement inhibits selecting, the user can turn off the pulsating blinking with [control-F4].
›All	All of the blinking object is included in the boundary.
›Partial	A portion of the blinking object is included in the boundary.

Consider portion 1-2 of blinking line L in Figure 10.1. The user selects *Partial*, picks a point M between 1 and 2 to select portion 1-2 (instead of 3-4), then precisely selects (snaps) and picks points 1 and 2 (not 7) to define the endpoints of the portion.

When L is picked while selecting portion 3-4, VersaCAD beeps and displays a message indicating line L has already been selected.

■ Menu Commands

Hatch›New
  Pick
  Group Pick

  Boundary
  Inquire
  Hatch
  Fill

  Delete
  Where
  List

  Size
  Calculate

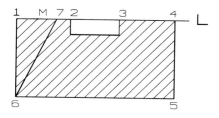

Figure 10.1

	This message can be ignored since the user is now selecting 3-4. At a later time, this message could indicate completion of the boundary.
›*Unpick*	Used when a previously selected boundary object is to be removed or have its endpoints reselected. When the object begins blinking, VersaCAD displays the "already picked" message. Selecting *Unpick* removes this message. An *Unpick* selection on an already unpicked object is ignored. A previously unpicked blinking object can again be picked by selecting *All* or *Partial*.
›*Quit*	Selected when *Pick* is finished.
Group Pick	Picks all the objects that are in the current group.
Boundary	Checks boundaries of the hatch area for closure. If no closure, VersaCAD calculates closure lines.
Inquire	Blinks each object portion of the current hatch boundary. Used to verify boundary object selection before hatching. If more objects need to be picked (or unpicked), user can again select *Pick*. Otherwise user selects *Hatch*.
Hatch	Hatches the current area. Four additional inputs are required (see Figure 10.2): *Spacing, Shift, Angle, Number*.

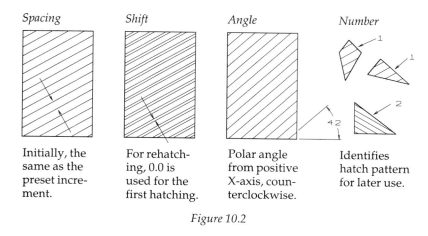

Spacing	Shift	Angle	Number
Initially, the same as the preset increment.	For rehatching, 0.0 is used for the first hatching.	Polar angle from positive X-axis, counterclockwise.	Identifies hatch pattern for later use.

Figure 10.2

Fill	Fills the hatch area with predefined hatching (refer to Figure 10.2). The user selects either *Fill* or *Hatch*. *Fill* will be more fully described after the next two hatch drawings.
Delete	Deletes a set of hatch lines by hatch number. Deleted hatching cannot later be undeleted. Instead, the boundary will have to be recreated.
Where	The user enters a hatch number. The lines with this number will blink in turn. To stop the blinking, the user can press [enter].
List	Displays all hatch numbers associated with the drawing, together with the number of individual lines having that hatch number.
Size	Increases the size of memory usually allocated for hatching.
Calculate	Calculates the area of the current boundary.

Note: To find the *hatch number* of a set of hatch lines, from the DRAFTING menu select *Inquire›Objects›*pick a hatch line› *Hatch*. A hatch number is displayed.

To *change a property* (a color, for example) of a hatch line set (you must know the hatch number beforehand), select *Group› Build›New›Yes›Objects›Lines›Hatch only›*key in the hatch number›*[enter]. Quit* to the GROUP menu, then select *Properties› Color›*key in the color number›*[enter]›Update*.

❏ DRAWING: HATCH-1

1. Execute Vcad and select *Drafting*.

2. Draw a front view and a full-section right-side view, including a border (no dimensions) of the object shown in Figure 10.3. First make a freehand sketch on paper of the two views and plan your method for drawing. You will need to decide the *Base, Units, Increment,* and *Grid*.

3. Your finished drawing should show thin section lines and centerlines and thicker outlines.

4. Plot and submit.

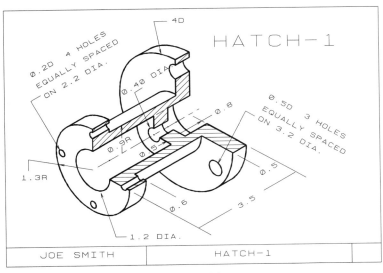

Figure 10.3

❏ DRAWING: ASSEMBLY

Note: The drawings for this exercise can be found in Figures 10.4 and 10.5.

1. Execute Vcad and select *Drafting*.

2. Sketch freehand on paper, then draw a full-section view of the assembled Jennifer pully, whose parts are shown in Figures 10.4 and 10.5. Dimensions not required.

3. Save as HATCH-2. Plot and submit.

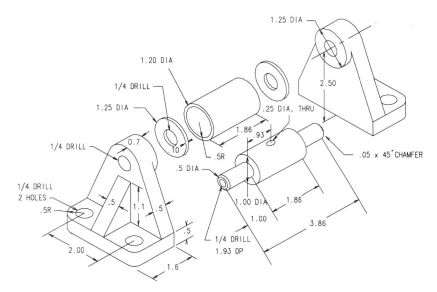

Figure 10.4

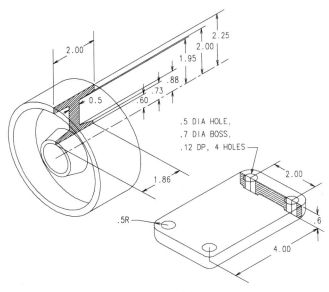

Figure 10.5

HATCH FILLS

Fill is used in lieu of *Hatch* after the hatch boundary has been picked and calculated. After reading the menu items below, draw three or four triangles. Fill them with different patterns.

■ **Menu Commands**

Hatch›Types
     Fill›Fill types
          Scale
          Rotation
          Number

Menu Item	Comment
Types	Displays the names of the fill patterns.
	VersaCAD currently has sixteen types of fill patterns (see Figure 10.6). This number can be increased by using customizing methods not discussed here. The fill patterns and names are shown below.
Fill	Selects a fill pattern. User is queried for the following:
›*Fill type*	The user keys in a pattern name (for example, steel).
›*Scale*	The user keys in a number to change the pattern size (for example, 2.0 to double the size).
›*Rotation*	The user rotates the pattern by keying in an angle.
›*Number*	The user keys in a hatch number for the fill pattern (which defaults to the next number in sequence).

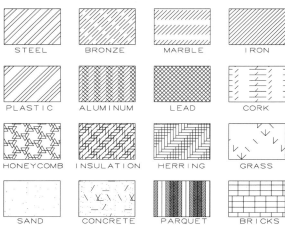

Figure 10.6
FILL PATTERNS

CHAPTER 11

Plotting

OBJECTIVES

- *To plot by using plot specifications rather than by default.*

- *To define plot boundaries and to plot portions of a display.*

- *To plot at various plot-paper sizes.*

CHAPTER CONTENTS

Plotter Specification

Exercise: Plotter Specification

Exercise: Plotter Specification Examples

Drawing: Plotter Specification

PLOTTER SPECIFICATION

You have been using *Output›Plotter›[enter]›[enter]›[enter]* to plot the monitor's graphics area onto plot paper as large as possible. If you wish to plot a different area, to use a different scale, or to confine the plot to a specific boundary on the plot paper, then select nondefault *Output›Specs*.

Menu Item	Comment
Window	The plot window (area to be plotted) is displayed as a rectangle within the graphics area (see Figure 11.1). Initially the plot window is the same size as the graphics area. The user selects *Window* to change the plot window's size, shape, or location. The objects within the plot window are the only objects that will be plotted.
Boundary	On plot paper, the **clip area** is the area beyond which plotting will not occur because of the limitations of the plotting device (see Figure 11.2). If a plotter is signalled to plot a line that extends out of the clip area, the plotter will plot the line until it reaches the clip boundary, where the line will end.
	The **plot boundary** is a rectangle within the clip area (see Figure 11.3). Objects in the plot window on the monitor are plotted within the plot boundary on the plot paper. Initially the origin of the plot boundary coincides with the origin of the clip area. The user selects *Boundary* mainly to center the boundary within the clip area, although the boundary could be placed anywhere within the clip area.
Factor	Used to scale what is to be plotted. Factor = 1.00 is the default.

> Scale = inches on paper/units on screen
> Factor = boundary size/window size

■ **Menu Commands**

Output›Specs›Window
  Boundary
  Factor

  Maximum

  Get
  Save
  Delete
  List

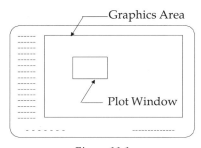

Figure 11.1
MONITOR

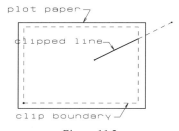

Figure 11.2

The user selects *Factor* to make the plot boundary fit in the clip area.

Maximum   The user selects *Maximum* to obtain the length and width of the clip area from the plotter (for those plotters capable of responding), so that the user can determine whether the plot boundary will fit within the clip area. The table below shows the plot boundaries obtained from an HP7475 plotter by selecting *Maximum*. Other plotters would have similar clip boundaries.

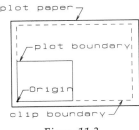

Figure 11.3

Paper	Metric Size	Customary Size	Clip Boundary			
			Left	Right	Bottom	Top
8½ × 11"	A4	A	0"	9.8135	0"	7.0658
11 × 17"	A3	B	0"	14.9166	0"	9.8135

Get
Save
Delete
List

A **plot specification** is a set of instructions that determine the plot window, plot boundary, and factor. Previous specifications can be retrieved for modification. New ones can be saved. If a new specification is saved as SAMPLE, the user can then plot using this spec by quitting to the OUTPUT menu, then selecting *Plotter›[enter]›[enter]›SAMPLE*.

The Plot Window

Plot Window, Plot Boundary, and Factor are interrelated. The shape (height-width ratio) of the window and boundary are *always* the same. Changing the shape of one correspondingly changes the shape of the other. Their sizes (widths) may differ, however, depending on the value of the Factor. The initial Factor equals 1 and the initial size and shape of both window and boundary are the same as the graphics area.

■ **Menu Commands**
Output›Specs›Window›
Move
Scale
Unpro-
portional

Place |

Menu Item	Comment
Move	Moves the lower left corner of the plot window to where the cursor is (see Figure 11.4). Sometimes a portion of the plot window is then out of the graphics area, but all of the window will still plot.
Scale	Scales (changes the size of) the plot window (see Figure 11.5). The lower left corner of the plot window remains fixed. The size changes as the cursor moves.
Unproportional	Reshapes the window (see Figure 11.6). The default shape of the plot window is the same shape as the graphics area. Reshaping is convenient when a user wishes to change the plot window so as to exclude objects from the plot.
Place	Places plot window as is, so the cursor can be moved without moving the plot window. The user then selects *Move, Scale,* or *Unproportional* to jump the plot window to the cursor.

Figure 11.4

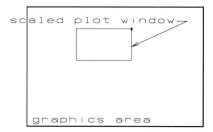

Figure 11.5

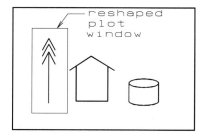

Figure 11.6

❑ EXERCISE: PLOTTER SPECIFICATION

To create a specification, the usual process is to (a) define the plot window; (b) define the plot boundary or factor; (c) change the plot boundary so the plot is centered (if you want it centered); and (d) *Save* the specs, *Quit,* then select *Plotter› [enter]›[enter]* and name the specs.

1. Execute Vcad and select *Drafting.* Without making a drawing, select *Output›Specs.*

2. Observe the SPECS menu (at the top left of the screen).

3. Observe the plot window, which usually shows as a rectangle in the graphics area. However, one object overlays another by blanking the shared pixels. Since the initial plot window is the graphics area, the boundaries of the graphics area confusingly disappear when *Output›Specs* is first selected. Fortunately they will reappear when the plot window is moved.

4. Observe the plot boundary. The default plot boundary is equal to the values shown in *Units›Base*. To verify this, *Quit* to the DRAFTING menu. Select *Units›Base* and create a 20-inch base. Return to *Output›Specs* and notice the new default plot boundary.

5. Observe the factor. The default factor is one.

6. Create a plot window. Select *[F6]›Increment›1›Quit* so the cursor will move to integer points only. Select *Window›Move* and move the lower left corner of the plot window to (3, 3). Select *Scale*, then *Unproportional*, and make a 2-inch wide, 10-inch tall plot window. Press the mouse button to record it. When VersaCAD asks "Recalculate Boundary or Factor?" select *Boundary*. (Either could be chosen since they will be changed in the next step.)

7. Assume you wish to plot at ⅜ inch = 1 inch. Select *Factor* along with ⅜ inch on paper, 1 inch on screen. When asked "Recalculate Boundary or Window?" select *Boundary* (we already recorded the plot window in the previous paragraph). The new boundary will be calculated. If the plot boundary is larger than the clip area of your plotter, you'll have to change the window or the factor. If the plot boundary fits within the clip boundary, then the usual practice is to select *Boundary* and center the plot boundary within the clip boundary. Assume you need to make no changes. Press the mouse button to record the size, shape and location of the plot window.

8. Save your specs under the name SAMPLE. *Quit* back to OUTPUT. Your next step would be to select *Plotter›[enter]›[enter]›Sample*; however, since we have nothing to plot, don't take this last step.

9. End of exercise.

❏ EXERCISE: PLOTTER SPECIFICATION EXAMPLES

1. One-fourth scale: User wishes to plot the current graphics area (Base = 20) at one-fourth scale.

Define the plot window: Select *Output›Specs.* No need to select *Window* since we are using the default plot window.

Define the factor: Select *Factor 1" on paper, 4" on screen.* Choose boundary for recalculation, since we don't want to change the current plot window. The new plot boundary values will be:

Left: 0   Bottom: 0

Right: 5   Top: 3.5

Center the plot: Select *Boundary.* Key in *Left (9.8 - 5)/2;* Right will automatically change to 7.4. *Select Bottom (7.0 - 3.5)/2;* Top will automatically change to 5.25. The plot will be centered (see Figure 11.7). Save specs.

Nothing to plot. *Quit* to DRAFTING menu.

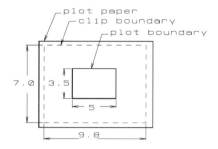

Figure 11.7

2. A-size unproportional: User wishes to plot a portion of the graphics area as large as possible on A-size paper. Centering is unnecessary.

Define the plot window: Select *Output›Specs›Window.* Select *Move, Scale,* and *Unproportional* to create a plot window surrounding an imaginary tall, thin pine tree in the center of the graphic area. Do not pick until the desired plot window has been created and located. Select boundary to be recalculated.

Define the factor: For maximum size on A-size plot paper, the boundary top should read approximately 7 inches. Assume it reads 20 inches, which is much too large. To change the boundary top to 7 inches, select *Factor 7" on paper, 20" on screen.* Allow the boundary to be recalculated—the boundary top should read 7 inches. Save specs. Nothing to plot.

3. B-size: User wishes to plot the top-right quarter of the current graphics area on B-size paper as large as possible.

Define the plot window: Select *Output›Specs›Window.* Move cursor to the middle of the graphics area. Scale the window so the plot window is roughly in the top-right quarter. Press the mouse button to record. Choose *Boundary* to recalculate with

Factor still default 1. The plot window length and width (Xw, Yw) are displayed. Save the specs as TEST2.

Define the plot boundary: Turn the plotter on. At the plotter, set to B-size. Return to station. Select *Maximum*, and the clip limits (Xc, Yc) will be displayed. Choose to recalculate either. Record the clip limits on a piece of paper (see Figure 11.8).

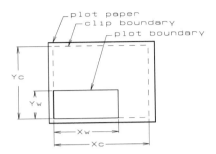

Figure 11.8

Select *Get›TEST2.* To fill up the clip area, the factor will have to be changed to the smaller of Yc/Yw and Xc/Xw (see Figure 11.9). Change the factor to its correct value and choose to recalculate the boundary. (Don't touch the window—its size has already been determined.)

Center the plot: Assuming centering is required in the Y direction, select *Boundary›left 0, right Xc, bottom (Yc-Ywnew)/2.* The top will be recalculated to (Ywnew + (Yc-Ywnew))/2 (see Figure 11.10).

Save the specs: Save the specs again as TEST2. *Quit.* There is nothing to plot. At the plotter, change back to A-size paper.

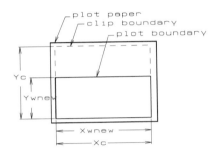

Figure 11.9

4. End of exercise.

❑ DRAWING: PLOTTER SPECIFICATION

1. Execute Vcad and select *Filer›dRive›F:DRAW›Get›BRACK-ET›dRive›B:* Put a border and title on the drawing. Add the comment: "SCALE: 5/8 SIZE." Plot the drawing centered on 8½-by-11-inch paper. Shrink the border along with the drawing.

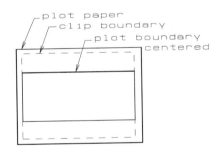

Figure 11.10

2. Select *Filer›dRive›F:DRAW›Get›CABIN›dRive›B:* Draw a 40-foot-wide-by-30-foot-high rectangle around the cabin. Plot this rectangle approximately centered on 11-by-17-inch plot paper so that the base of the rectangle is 11 inches.

3. Select *Filer›dRive›F:DRAW›Get›ISOFLNG›dRive›B:* Create a rectangle around the front and right-side views. Using *Unproportional*, place the plot window over the rectangle. Plot the drawing centered on 24-by-36-inch paper as large as possible, and submit.

CHAPTER 12

Libraries

OBJECTIVES

- *To define a library.*
- *To create symbols and place them in the library.*
- *To use symbols in the library while creating a drawing.*

CHAPTER CONTENTS

Defining a Library

Placing Symbols in a Library

Exercise: Library and Overlay Creation

Using Symbols in a Drawing

Exercise: Adding Symbols

Moving an Attached Group

Drawing: Sym-1

DEFINING A LIBRARY

A **library** is a file containing drawings that may be used as objects in the current drawing. A **symbol** is a drawing that has been placed in a library.

With the *Library* option, a user may create a library in the current directory and copy drawings from the current directory into the library. Later, with the option *Add›Symbol,* the user may copy symbols from the active library into this drawing.

Menu Item	Comment
Make	The user keys in a name (up to eight characters) for a new library. The user also keys in the number of symbol locations (cells) needed for the new library. You can use as many as one thousand symbols in a library.
Delete	The user keys in the name of the library to be deleted from the current directory.
List	Lists the names of the libraries in the current directory.
Ext-list	Displays the libraries list with more details.
dRive	The user keys in the pathname to be used to search for a library.
Active	The user keys in the name of the library to be the active library.
Overlay	Creates a symbol table (overlay) as a drawing, which can then be plotted and used for subsequent reference for future drawings. Initially the user must have an empty workfile, the correct current drive, and the correct active library. The user then selects *Library› Overlay.*
Symbol	Adds or deletes a symbol in the current library.
Crunch	Repeated symbol deletions and additions to a library can fill it up. *Crunch* removes all deleted symbols, allowing room for more additions.

■ **Menu Commands**

Library›Make
Delete
List
Ext-list
dRive
Active

Overlay
Symbol
Crunch

PLACING SYMBOLS IN A LIBRARY

Menu Item	Comment
Add	The user keys in the name of a drawing in the current directory and the number of an empty cell. The drawing then becomes a symbol in the current library.
Delete	The user keys in the cell number of a symbol to be deleted from the current library.
Handle	The user keys in the cell number of a symbol whose handle is to be changed. VersaCAD then makes an enlarged drawing of the symbol and the cursor is used to select a new handle. The new handle location is stored in the library along with the symbol.
	A symbol may have only one handle, originally the first endpoint of the first object of the symbol. To change the handle of a symbol that is already part of a drawing, the user selects *Modify›Find›Handle* (not *Library›Symbol›Handle*).
Outline	The user keys in the cell number of the symbol whose outline is to be defined. *Yes* is selected for each blinking object that is to be part of the symbol outline. *No* is selected for each blinking object that is not to be part of the outline. This new outline information is stored in the library along with the symbol. When a symbol is placed in a drawing, its outline is part of the symbol record. VersaCAD uses this outline information when the user selects *Switches›Outline›Yes* to speed up the redrawing of a drawing containing numerous symbols.
List	Lists the names and cell numbers of symbols in the current library.

■ **Menu Commands**

Library›Symbol›Add
Delete
Handle
Outline
List

❑ EXERCISE: LIBRARY AND OVERLAY CREATION

In this exercise, you'll create a library and place symbols in it. (This exercise is required for the last drawing in this chapter.)

1. Execute Vcad and get your previously drawn GROUP-MAC; erase the right half of the drawing.

2. Save GROUPS as DRAWINGS: Move the inductor (select *Group›Move*) to the open area on the right. Select *Modify›Find* and scale the bottom line of the inductor to the same size as the top line of the inductor (see Figure 12.1). Select *Filer›Save› Group›INDUCTOR* to save the inductor. In a similar manner save other parts of the drawing (see Figure 12.2).

3. Save a big group: Get a fresh GROUPMAC drawing. Use *Group›Build›New›Yes›Inverse* and shrink GROUPMAC to one-tenth its size. Save it as BIG.

4. Exit Vcad. In DOS type DIR [enter] to verify that all your drawings are in the current directory.

5. Create symbols: Execute Vcad and select *Library›Make› PARTS›12* to make a parts library with twelve empty cells. Select *Library›Active›Parts*. Select *Library›Symbol›Add›INDUC-TOR to cell 1*. Add the other parts similarly. Place BIG in cell 12.

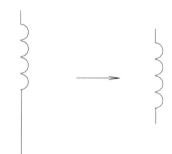

Figure 12.1

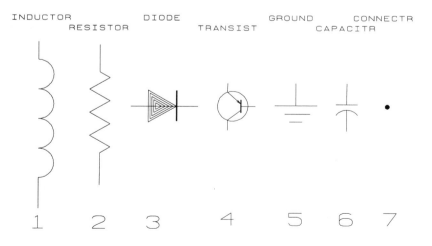

Figure 12.2

6. Create a symbol outline: Select *Outline›12*—the symbol in cell 12 will be displayed. Move cursor and blink each object in turn, selecting *No* for every object except one rectangle of the border and the title GROUPMAC. Later, this will allow you to represent this symbol in either its full or an abbreviated form.

7. Create an overlay: Select *Filer›New›Yes*. Overlays must be created from empty workfiles. Select *Library›Active›Parts*. Select *Library›Overlay›4›3›[enter]›[enter]*. Place your name in the lower right corner of the drawing.

8. Plot the overlay: This is for your reference only, not for submission.

9. End of exercise.

USING SYMBOLS IN A DRAWING

After a symbol number is selected, the symbol appears in the drawing area and tracks the cursor. The symbol can be rotated or imaged, then picked.

Menu Item	Comment
Rotate	Rotates the symbol by the preset rotation angle amount.
Image	Images the symbol about the Y-axis.
Outline	Abbreviates the symbol to its outline instead of its full display.
Handle	Redefines a symbol's handle (a symbol has only one handle).
Factor	Changes the size of the symbol (for example, 0.5 is half size).
Global	Changes the properties of the symbol to the current preset values.
Cut	Cuts (breaks and trims) a line when a symbol is placed to overlay the line.
Erase	Erases the previously placed symbol.

■ **Menu Commands**

Add›Symbol›Symbol num›
Rotate
Image
Outline
Handle
Factor
Global
Cut
Erase

❏ EXERCISE: ADDING SYMBOLS

This exercise gives you the experience of scaling a symbol prior to its placement in a drawing. It also demonstrates the value of having an abbreviation (outline) for a symbol.

1. Execute Vcad. Use a base of 15 and make PARTS the active library.

2. Select *Add›Symbol›Symbol num›1*. Move the cursor into the graphics area so the symbol can be seen. Since the symbol was saved using a base of 30 and since the base is now 15, the symbol appears double size. A single symbol can be factored by selecting *Factor*. Instead proceed as follows: *Quit* to the DRAFTING menu. Select *Units›Symbol›0.5*. All subsequent symbols will be factored. Draw a few symbols for practice.

3. Outline: Select *Add›Symbol›Symbol num›12*. Notice the sluggish tracking. Place two symbols, then select *Outline*. Notice more speed in tracking. Place two more, then *Quit* to DRAFTING.

4. Fast redraw: Select *sKetch* to redraw the outlines as full symbols. Since resketching numerous symbols is often a slow process, select *Switches›Outline›Yes›sKetch* to speed up the process.

5. End of exercise.

MOVING AN ATTACHED GROUP

In the next drawing, you will be drawing a circuit diagram. First you'll draw the diagram without symbols. However, when you place a number of vertical and horizontal lines by eye, the diagram will probably end up out of proportion. You can correct most of the proportions by selecting *Group›Move› Attached*, and to a lesser extent *Construct›Extend* and *Modify› Scale*.

A group is built using *Fence* (must use *Fence*). All objects within or partially within the fence become part of the group. Then, when you select *Group›Move›Attached*, the outside endpoint of any line partially within the fence remains in place and the line stretches or shrinks to accommodate the move.

The diagrams in Figure 12.3 demonstrate the effect of using *Group›Move›Attached*. In each case the group is *Move›Attached* from point 1 to point 2.

■ **Menu Commands**
Group›Move›Attached *X-axis* *Y-axis* *Free*

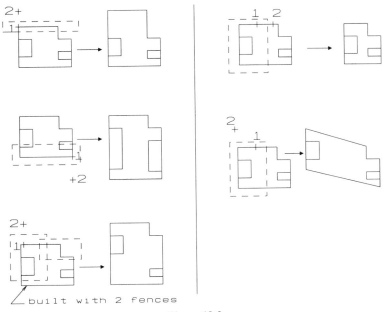

Figure 12.3

❑ Drawing: Sym-1

Note: This drawing is shown in Figure 12.4.

1. Execute Vcad. Select a base of 30. (Merge in the border after the drawing is complete.)

2. Wiring: Draw all the wiring without any symbols inserted. Distances between wiring will probably be all out of proportion on your first attempt. To bring into proportion, make judicious use of *Group›Move›Attached.*

3. Symbols: Place your PARTS library overlay next to the computer where you can see the symbol numbers that correspond to each symbol.

Select *Library›Active›PARTS.* Select *Add›Symbol›Symbol num›4.* Since the symbol appears too large, press [escape], then select *Units›Symbol›0.6.*

Select *Add›Symbol›Symbol num›4.* Rotate the symbol. Select *Cut* and place the transistor symbols on the drawing using *[F2]›Snap.*

Place the rest of the symbols on the drawing. To draw the long inductor, explode an inductor symbol that has been placed at the top part of the long inductor location. Then use *Group›Copy.*

Use *Window›In* and *Modify›Find* to clean up any inaccurate symbol locations.

4. Merge in border (you may first want to change the base).

5. Plot and submit.

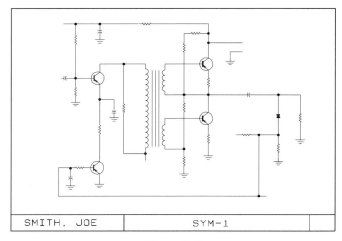

Figure 12.4

CHAPTER 13

Digitizers

OBJECTIVES

- *To expand digitizer use beyond that of cursor movement in the graphics area.*

- *To set up the digitizer to use an overlay.*

- *To use the symbols in a digitizer's overlay to make a drawing.*

CHAPTER CONTENTS

Digitizers

Exercise: Overlay Sheet

Multilines

Drawing: Overlay Usage

DIGITIZERS

A digitizer is an input device that can sense the location of a probe within a rectangular area. Most digitizers use a grid of wires embedded within their rectangular tablet surface, together with a wire coil in a stylus (a pencil-like probe). Electrical interaction between grid and probe is used to sense the location of the stylus on the tablet.

A common way to use the digitizer is to define a rectangular area on the tablet in the same shape as the graphics area on the monitor screen. When the user places the stylus within this rectangular area, the digitizer sends the coordinates of the location to the VersaCAD program. The VersaCAD program locates the cursor in the graphics area of the monitor screen accordingly.

Tablet Usage

In addition to cursor location, the stylus can be used as a pointer. You can set up four different types of rectangular areas on a tablet and use the stylus as appropriate. The four areas are:

1. Drawing area	Stylus location determines cursor location
2. Library area	Stylus location determines symbol selection
3. Menu area	Stylus location determines menu item selection
4. Macro command area	Stylus location determines which macro to execute

The tablet can be set up with just one area—for example, a drawing area—or it can be set up with many areas and with more than one area of a given type. For example, two different library areas could be defined: one for electrical and one for mechanical symbols. Or four different drawing areas could be set up: areas for top, front, side, and isometric views to help create three-dimensional drawings by tracing.

Setting Up Areas

When VersaCAD executes, a default drawing area and a default menu area are in place on the tablet (see Figure 13.1). To verify this, pass the stylus over the drawing area and you'll see cursor movement on the screen; pass the stylus over the menu area and menu items will be highlighted.

To define new areas, select *iNput›Overlay›Area›Add*. See the following chart for associated submenus:

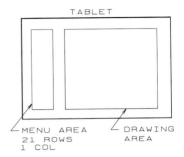

Figure 13.1

Menu 1	**Menu 2**	**Menu 3**	**Menu 4**
iNput›Digitizer			
Mouse			
Keyboard			
Plotter			
Overlay› →	*Area›* →	*Add›* →	*Drawing*
Alt menu	*Get*	*Delete*	*Menu*
	Save	*Replace*	*Library*
	Delete	*Tracing*	*Command*
	List	*Inquire*	
	Overlay		

To set up an area on the tablet, from menu 4 select the type of area, then with the stylus, locate on the tablet the upper left, lower left, and lower right corners. From menu 3, you can select *Tracing* and then key in a scale for an existing drawing area. The drawing area can then be used to trace an existing drawing on paper into the workfile. From menu 2, you can select *Overlay* to display the existing setup of rectangles (overlay setup) for the tablet. This setup can be altered, plotted, and then taped down onto the tablet so that you can see where the rectangular areas are.

❑ EXERCISE: OVERLAY SHEET

The overlay sheet created from this exercise will be used in the next drawing.

1. From a digitizer station, execute Vcad and select *Drafting*.

2. The default overlay setup: When you execute Vcad, two rectangular areas are set up on the tablet (see Figure 13.1).

Run the stylus up and down the menu area on the tablet to highlight different menu items. Experiment by selecting *Add* (select by pushing the stylus down when *Add* is highlighted), then select *Line*. Move the stylus to the drawing area and draw a few lines by pushing the stylus down to pick a point. Draw a few objects to get the feel of using the stylus.

Select *iNput›Overlay›Area›Inquire*. When the stylus is in the menu area, the display shows the area name (no name for now), the boundary of the rectangle, the type (M for menu area), the number of rows and columns, and the number of the current menu item. Similar information is shown when you move the stylus to the drafting area. *D* is an abbreviation for drafting. There is only one position in the drafting area.

Quit to *Drafting*, then select *Filer›New* to clear the screen. Select *iNput›Overlay›Overlay›No›No* to see a picture of the current rectangular area setup, then select *Filer›New* to remove the picture.

3. Create a new overlay setup:

Select *iNput›Overlay›Area›Delete*. Delete the two default areas. Use *Area›Inquire* and move the stylus around the tablet to verify that all areas have been deleted.

Select *Filer›dRive›I:›Get›$WORKTAB›dRrive›B:* Plot $WORKTAB, then attach it to the tablet. You may have to tape it down.

Menu area: Create and name a new rectangular area by selecting *iNput›Overlay›Area›Add›Menu›Name›MENUAREA*, then locate the upper left, lower left, and lower right corners.

Drawing area: From *iNput›Overlay›Area*, select *Add›Drawing› Name›DRAWAREA*, then locate the drawing area corners. Select the drawing area boundary.

Library area: An existing library, DEMOLIB, is already stored on the hard disk. We will use a portion of it for our drawing. From DRAFTING, select *Library›dRive›F:LIB* to select the correct directory. Then select *iNput›Overlay›Area›Add›Library› DEMOLIB›6 rows, 2 cols*, and locate the library area corners. Define the library area boundary. Save this overlay setup under the name NEWOVLAY. The upper left, lower left, and lower right corners used to save it must encompass all your previously defined rectangular areas.

4. Create an overlay sheet: From DRAFTING, select *Filer› New›Yes* to clear the graphics area, then select *iNput›Overlay› Overlay›Yes›Yes* to create an overlay sheet. Add the titles DRAWING AREA, MENU AREA, LIB. AREA (DEMOLIB), your name, and the letters A, B, and C. Plot the overlay sheet. Exit to DOS and key in DIR to see the filename NEWOV-LAY.TAB, which contains the overlay setup you have just defined. Execute Vcad, then select *Drafting* to verify that the current overlay setup is the default setup (two rectangular areas).

Place your new overlay sheet securely on the tablet (tape it if necessary). It doesn't have to be placed precisely where the other overlay sheet was placed because you will be defining its new location to VersaCAD. Select *iNput›Overlay›Get› NEWOVLAY*. Define the boundary by picking the corners marked A, B, and C. You are now ready to use this new overlay to make a drawing.

MULTILINES

By selecting *Add›Multiline*, a user can draw a set of parallel lines as though a single line were being drawn. Although figures 13.2–13.5 show only 4 lines, the concept applies to up to 255 lines. (Please note that the menu items below are presented in the order that they are used.)

Menu Item	Comment
Numlines	Selects the number of lines. A two-line multiline is the default.
Width	Changes the width distance between lines.
Offset	Changes the meaning of *Width* (see Figure 13.2).
Pivot	Corresponds to a line's first endpoint.
Handle	Corresponds to a line's second endpoint. The default locations of the pivot and handle are at the center as shown in Figure 13.3. When *Pivot* is repeatedly selected both the pivot and handle sequence through center, lower, and upper locations. When *Handle* is selected, only the handle is sequenced.

■ Menu Commands

FOR PIVOT:

Add›Multiline›Single
Offset
Join
Width
Numlines
Erase

FOR HANDLE:

Add›Multiline›Marker
Template

X-axis
Y-axis
Rotate
Free

Detach
Single

Pivot
Handle
Caps

Offset
Join
Lock
Width
Numlines
Erase

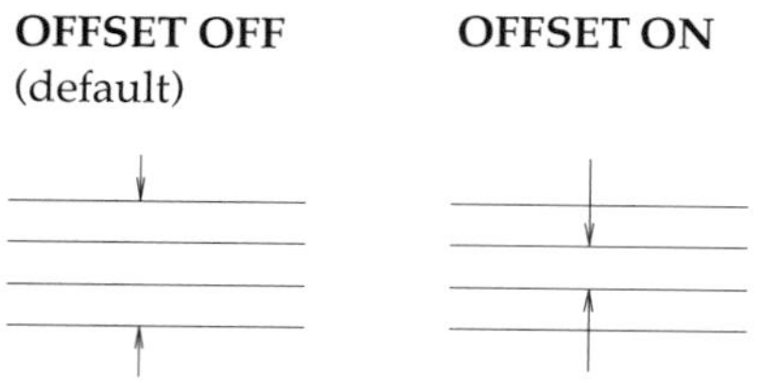

OFFSET OFF
(default)

OFFSET ON

Figure 13.2

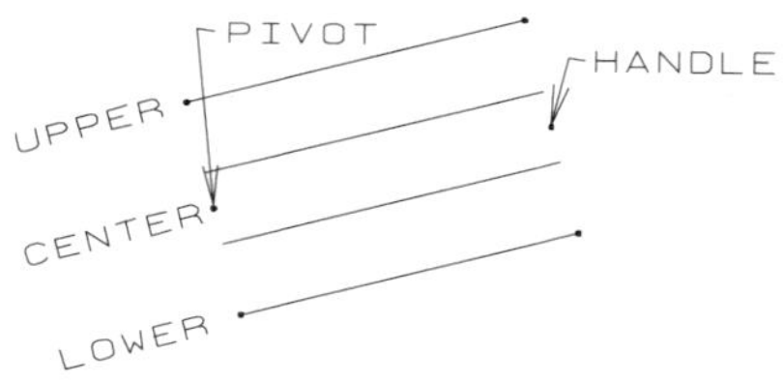

Figure 13.3

Join	Joins current multiline to an object (see Figure 13.4).	**JOIN OFF** **JOIN ON**
Lock	The lock option is displayed only after *Join* is changed to *JOIN*. Locks the multiline in place to allow easier joining. The user picks any point on the object that the multiline is to join, and the intersection becomes a joined intersection.	*Figure 13.4*
Caps	Sequences through the various cap options shown in Figure 13.5.	

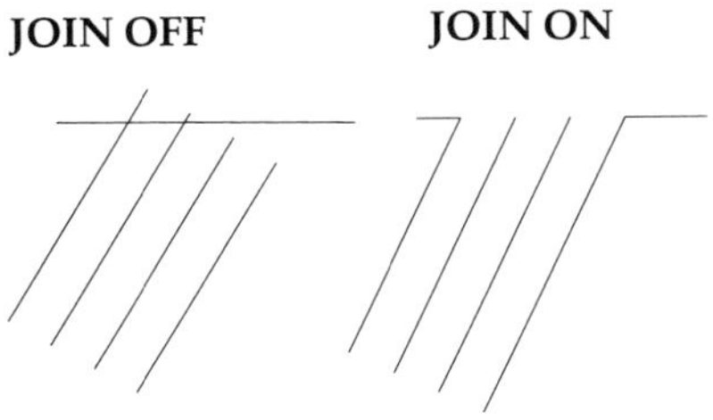

NO   **START**   **END**   **BOTH**
CAP   **CAP**   **CAP**   **CAP**

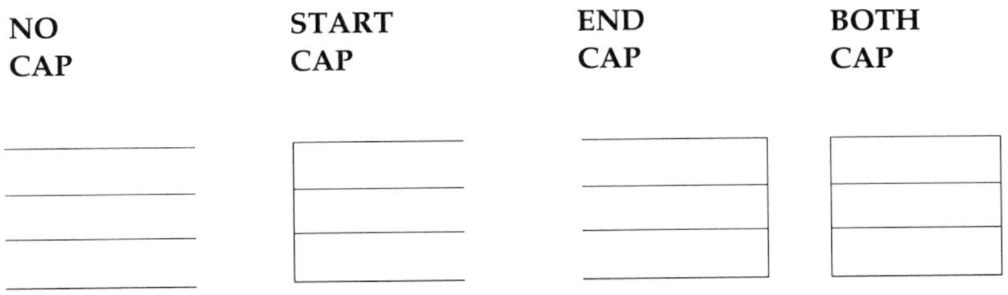

Figure 13.5

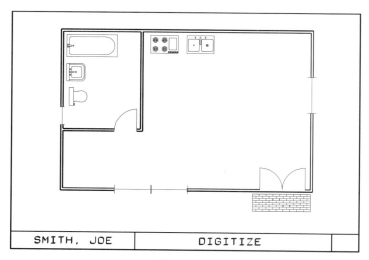

Figure 13.6

❏ DRAWING: OVERLAY USAGE

Note: This drawing is shown in Figures 13.6 and 13.7.

1. Execute Vcad and select *Units›Units›Feet*. Using a base of 30 and leaving the border for later, select *Add›Multiline* and draw four multilines to form a rectangle that just about fills the screen. This rectangle represents a floor plan of the walls of a structure. If the last line joins the first line sloppily, use *Construct›Extend* to fix the corner.

2. Select *Library›dRive›F:LIB›Active›DEMOLIB*. From DRAFTING, select *Add›Symbol* (you do not have to select *Symbol Num* if you use a digitizer). Pick the bathtub on your NEWOVLAY sheet with the stylus, then place it by eye. Similarly, pick the wash basin, rotate it, and place it. Pick and place the toilet.

3. Using *Multiline›JOIN*, draw the inside rectangular wall.

4. Select *Add›Symbol›CUT*. Pick the outside door (which is symbol number 2). Place it using *[F2]›Object›EQUATION* on the outside wall. Similarly, *Image* then place the bathroom door. Place the stove and kitchen sink.

5. Select *Units›Base* and change to a 40-foot base. Use *Group* to place the floor plan more conveniently. Add the brick porch (which is two symbol 8s, one of them rotated 180 degrees). Add the bathroom window (symbol 10). Select *Factor* to double the size of symbol 10, then place the other windows.

6. Merge in a border.

7. Plot and submit.

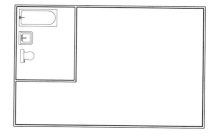

Figure 13.7

CHAPTER 14

The 3D Scene World

OBJECTIVE

- *To introduce the concepts and power of 3D drafting.*

CHAPTER CONTENTS

INTRODUCTORY CONCEPTS

If you execute Vcad and select *Drafting*, points will be located using two X-Y coordinate dimensions. If you select *Modeling* instead, points will be located using three X-Y-Z coordinate dimensions. The 3D MODELING menus differ from the 2D DRAFTING menus. While there is some carryover of skills learned in 2D, the 3D concepts are quite different. Since 3D drafting is a complex subject, we'll cover only the major ideas here, while trying to give you a feeling of its power.

In 3D drafting, the **scene** is the volume used to locate the set of three-dimensional objects to be drawn. The scene workfile contains the data necessary to create any view of the scene. This scene workfile (V3D.WRK) is a different file from the 2D drafting workfile (V2D.WRK).

The **scene window** is a two-dimensional rectangular view of the scene as displayed in the graphics area of the monitor. The scene appears as 3D in the 2D scene window by being displayed in isometric or in three-point perspective (which is the default).

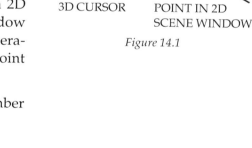

3D CURSOR   POINT IN 2D
                   SCENE WINDOW

Figure 14.1

For certain pick operations, the cursor is displayed as a 2D crosshair cursor that moves around within the scene window in a manner similar to the 2D drafting cursor. For most operations, though, the cursor is displayed as a 3D three-point perspective cursor (see Figure 14.1).

A single point in the 2D scene window can represent a number of points in the 3D scene (see Figure 14.2).

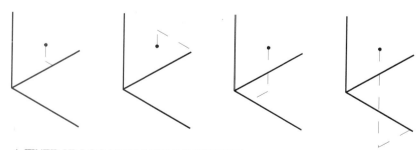

A FIXED 2D LOCATION COULD REPRESENT MANY 3D LOCATIONS.

Figure 14.2

Simply moving the cursor to a 2D point in the scene window may not move it to the desired 3D point in the scene. Therefore, the third direction needs to be considered.

In the lower right corner of the monitor screen, the **coordinate display** shows values for three coordinates: X, Y, and Z in that order. To control cursor movement, at least one of the coordinates is always highlighted (reverse video). A highlighted coordinate is "locked" and will not change as the cursor is moved. If the Y- and Z-axes are locked, for example, the cursor will move in the X direction only. Locking is more fully described in the next drawing.

Because a 3D scene is three-dimensional, it cannot be plotted. However, a scene window can be changed to a 2D drawing and then can be plotted or otherwise modified as any two-dimensional drawing is modified. (Note that in 2D drafting, a drawing is saved with a .2D filename extension; in 3D drafting, a scene workfile is saved with a .3D extension.

There are two reference lists for modeling at the end of this book. This chapter uses the SCENE WORLD reference list. The next chapter uses the CREATE WORLD reference list. Note the similarities and differences between these menus and the 2D drafting menus. Exercises in this chapter will help you gain familiarity with the SCENE WORLD menu items.

Scene Saving (3D)

Filer is selected to save a scene. The scene workfile is saved with a 3D extension, for example, FIRST.3D.

■ **Menu Commands**

Filer›Get
        Save
        Merge
        New

        Delete
        List
        Ext-list
        What
        dRive

Window Saving (2D)

Export is selected to save a scene window as a 2D drawing. The user selects *Wireframe, Backface, Hidden,* or *Ortho*. If *Hidden* is selected, the view is redisplayed with hidden lines removed, then saved with a 2D extension (for example, FIRST.2D). *Wireframe, Backface,* and *Ortho* will be described in a following section.

```
■ Menu Commands
─────────────────────
Export› Wireframe
        Backface
        Hidden
        Ortho

        Delete
        List
        Ext-list
        dRive
```

❑ DRAWING: 3D—A Study of Cursor Movement

Note: This drawing is shown in Figure 14.3.

1. Execute Vcad, select *Modeling* and the SCENE menu will be displayed.

2. 3D cursor: Move the cursor to the approximate center of the screen window. Select *[F5]›(cursor)* a few times to see how the cursor changes. Notice the 3D right-hand system of coordinate axes on the cursor.

3. Locking coordinates: Be sure that [numlock] is off. If it isn't, press the [numlock] key. Select *[control-F5]›Cursor* to set up the

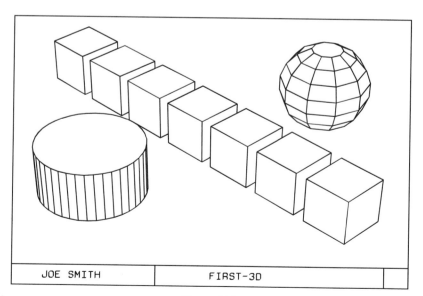

Figure 14.3

keypad for cursor movement. Select *Add›Box*, then alternately select 1, 2, or 3 on the numeric keypad to see X, Y, or Z highlighted. Move the cursor to verify that the highlighted coordinates remain locked as the other coordinates change. If the highlight begins to jiggle irritatingly, move the cursor a little to stop the jiggle.

With Y and Z locked notice that movement in the +X direction is isometric, toward the bottom right. After proper locking, the +Y and +Z directions also move isometrically.

4. Boxes: Select *Add›Box* again and pick its initial point at (0, 0, 0). Select *[F6]›Increment›1›Quit*. By locking and unlocking coordinates, move the cursor to pick the next point at (4, 4, 4). *Quit* back to the SCENE menu, select *Modify›Copy* (for now, do not use *Repeat*), and copy individually to make a total of seven boxes. Place the other first points five units apart along the X-axis with Y = 0 and Z = 0. *Quit* back to the SCENE menu.

5. Cylinder: Select *Add›Cylinder›Whole›Create›Length 4›Radius 4*. The cursor moves sluggishly because 3D tracking is slow. Press [F4] to turn off tracking. Notice in the bottom left of the screen that the *T* has been replaced by a dot. Place the cursor for the cylinder at (0, -12, 4). Pick the cylinder. Turn tracking back on. *Quit* to the ADD menu.

6. Sphere: Place cursor at (0, 14, 2) in preparation for drawing a sphere. Select *Sphere›Whole›Create›Radius 4*. Tracking consists of repeatedly displaying and erasing the sphere. Unlock the Z-axis and move the cursor a little. It may take ten seconds or more for the sphere to move. Press the [escape] key to stop the process. Be patient. The sphere will track through two on-off cycles before responding to the user. It takes time for VersaCAD to catch up (sometimes as long as a minute!).

Select *F6›Sides 10›Quit*. Select *Create›Radius 4*. Tracking is not quite as slow as it was. Turn off tracking and wait. Place cursor at (0, 14, 2) and pick the sphere. Turn tracking back on. *Quit* back to the SCENE menu.

7. Save: Select *Filer›Save›FIRST:* The file is saved as FIRST.3D. *Quit* to the SCENE menu. Select *Export›Hidden›FIRST* to save FIRST.2D. *Quit* to SCENE, then *eXit*. Do not save the 3D workfile.

8. 2D Drawing: Select *Drafting›Filer›Get›FIRST*. Using *Group›Build›New›Yes›Inverse*, move all the objects down a little in preparation for a border, then draw the border (don't try to merge in a border, the base size would surprise you).

9. Plot and submit.

10. From DOS, key in DIR to see the FIRST.3D and FIRST.2D files listed. Note that FIRST.3D is smaller than FIRST.2D—FIRST.3D contains only nine objects, whereas FIRST.2D contains many more.

3D OBJECTS

An object in a scene is either a primitive object or a created object. To create an object, select *Modeling›Create*, then use the CREATE menu items to create and join surfaces. Created objects will be examined in the next chapter.

A **primitive object** is one of the four predefined VersaCAD 3D objects: *Box, Cylinder, cOne,* and *Sphere*. Menu item *Add* is selected to draw a primitive.

Box

The box primitive is drawn by defining the X-Y-Z coordinates of its lower left corner, then the X-Y-Z coordinates of its upper right corner.

■ Menu Commands
Add›Box

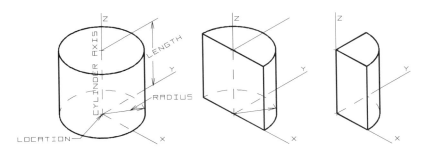

Figure 14.4

Cylinder

The cylinder primitive is drawn by defining its geometry, its orientation, and the location of the center of its base. A series of menus are displayed. The user selects menu items, then keys in responses to VersaCAD queries.

■ **Menu Commands**
Add›Cylinder

Menu Item	**Comment**
Whole *Half* *qUarter*	The user selects which type of cylinder is to be drawn: whole, half, or quarter (see Figure 14.4).
Create *Baseline* *Radius*	The user selects the type of cylinder to be drawn. Before selecting *Create*, the user selects *Baseline* or *Radius*, *Baseline* and *Radius*, or neither (see Figure 14.5).
	Select *Radius* and the menu item will change to uppercase (*RADIUS*). The user can then create a cylinder with base of Radius1 and a

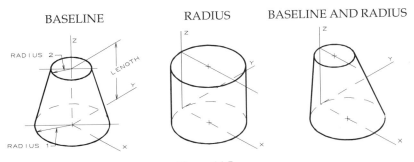

Figure 14.5

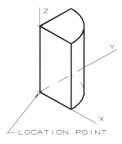
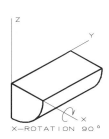
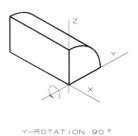

Figure 14.6

top of Radius2. Mathematicians would call the resulting figure a frustum of a cone, rather than a cylinder.

Select *Baseline* to display a cylinder with one edge just touching the edge of the Z-axis and with the center of the base on the X-axis one radius away from the cursor.

Select *Baseline* and *Radius* to create a cylinder (cone frustum) with the edge on the Z-axis as shown in Figure 14.5.

X-rotation
Y-rotation
Z-rotation

The cylinder can be rotated about its location point by an amount equal to a multiple of the rotation angle. The rotation angle is preset with *[F6]›Rotation*. Looking toward the positive direction of the axis selected, the cylinder will be rotated counter-clockwise (see Figure 14.6).

Cone

The cone is added in a manner similar to the cylinder.

Sphere

The sphere is added by locating its center and selecting its radius.

❏ EXERCISE: ROTATION

1. Execute Vcad and select *Modeling.* With [numlock] off, select *[control-F5]›Cursor* to set up the keypad for cursor movement. Preset *Increment 1, Sides 20* and *Rotation 90.*

2. Select *[F5]›long cursor*, then draw a quarter cylinder Length 6, Radius 3 located at (0, 0, 0). Visualize how the object would be displayed with one X-rotation, then select *X-rotation* to verify.

3. Visualize the next X-rotation, then verify. After selecting *X-rotation* four times, you should see the object in its original position.

4. Repeat this exercise for *Y-rotation* and *Z-rotation.* Remember to visualize how the object should be displayed on the next rotation, then rotate to verify your visualization.

5. End of exercise.

❑ DRAWING: 3D ROTATION

Note: This drawing is shown in Figure 14.7.

1. Execute Vcad and select *Modeling.* Select *[control-F5]›Cursor* to set up the keypad for cursor movement. Preset *Sides=10, Color 3, Increment 1.* In this drawing, you will move the cursor to locate objects rather than locating them with absolute coordinates.

2. Cylinders: Draw two cylinders of *Length 16, Radius 3,* located at (0, -8, 0) and (-8, 0, 0). Rotate them as shown in the drawing.

3. Sphere: Use *Color 4.* The quarter sphere is located at (-16, 0, 0). Visualize how it should be displayed initially, then what rotations are needed. Then draw it with *Radius 3.*

4. Cone frustum: Draw a red cylinder of *Length 8, Radius 1 = 3, Radius 2 = 1,* located at (16, 0, 0), and rotated as shown.

5. X-Y-Z line: Using *Color 5,* draw the axis lines shown. A line is not a primitive in 3D. Use cylinders of 0.1 radius to draw the axes shown in the drawing. Make the vertical axis twice the frustum height.

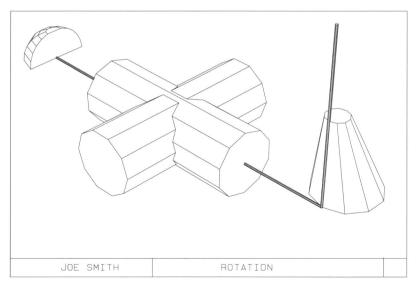

JOE SMITH	ROTATION	

Figure 14.7

6. Full visibility: Select *Filer›Save›ROTATION*. Select *Group›Build›New›Yes›Inverse›Quit*, then move the scene from the origin four units in the negative X direction so that all the objects will be visible.

7. Export the scene window to 2D. Save your 3D scene. Exit *Modeling* without *Keeping*.

When a scene window is exported, the pen number assigned to an object is the same as its color number. Create a border with title using *Pen 6*.

8. Plot and submit.

DISPLAY CHOICES

Wireframe: A box may be considered as the set of line segments that join its eight corners. The calculations necessary to display this wireframe box are relatively undemanding. The location of the projections of the eight points onto the projection plane are calculated; the lines are then drawn between these eight points. The redisplay is almost immediate.

All the edges of the box are displayed (see Figure 14.8). The disadvantage to the wireframe display is that the viewer is unable to determine if the view is of the top or the bottom of the box. The view sometimes appears to flipflop.

Hidden: A box may be considered as a set of six surfaces together with their edge intersections. When *Export›Hidden* is selected, the nonvisible edges disappear (see Figure 14.9). These edges can also be made dashed by selecting *Switches› Hidden*, so that the view loses its flipflop appearance (see Figure 14.10). The calculations for *Hidden* are quite demanding, however, and the wait is long before redisplay occurs.

■ **Menu Commands**
Export›Wireframe
Hidden
Backface

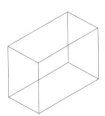

Figure 14.8
WIREFRAME

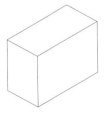

Figure 14.9
HIDDEN

Backface: If the three back faces of a box are not displayed and if visibility calculations are not made for the three front faces, the redisplay wait is minimal and the display for a single box is identical to the no-dash hidden display (see Figure 14.11). However, if two objects are displayed, a portion of a front face of one object may be behind the front face of a second object. Since all of a front face is displayed, some hidden lines will be displayed (compare Figures 14.12 and 14.13).

Generally, users work with the *Wireframe* display, occasionally using *Backface*; usually just before exporting, they may switch to *Hidden*.

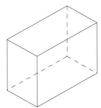

Figure 14.10
HIDDEN-DASH

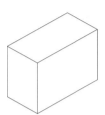

Figure 14.11
BACKFACE

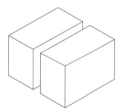

Figure 14.12
HIDDEN

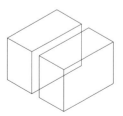

Figure 14.13
BACKFACE

VIEWS

The scene window can display either isometric or three-point perspective (the default) projections. The user may change the scene window display from one projection to the other by selecting *[F7]›Isometric* or *Perspective*.

Center of Interest

The coordinates of two points, the center of interest and the eyepoint, define a viewing direction for a scene window. The center of interest is a point in the scene whose default coordinates are (0, 0, 0) (see Figure 14.14). Its projection is always at the center of the scene window. Changing its coordinates changes the display. Figure 14.15 shows the display resulting from *[F7]›Camera›Center 0›-14›0*.

Eyepoint

The eyepoint is also a point in the scene. A ray from the eyepoint to the center of interest defines the viewing direction. Changing the eyepoint changes the coordinate directions. Figure 14.16 shows the display resulting from *[F7]›Camera›Eye› 50,-50,-50*.

> ■ **Menu Commands**
>
> *[F7]›Isometric*
>   *Perspective*
>
>   *Camera›Center*
>   *Eye*
>   *Get*
>   *Save*
>   *List*
>   *Delete*

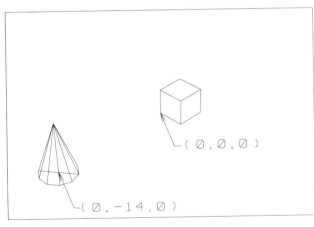

Figure 14.14
CENTER (0, 0, 0)   EYE (50, -50, 50)

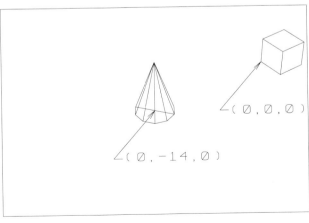

Figure 14.15
CENTER COORDINATE CHANGE (0, -14, 0)

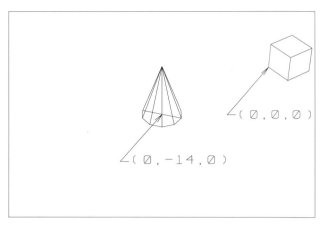

Figure 14.16
EYEPOINT COORDINATE CHANGE (50, -50, -50)

Saving the Viewing Direction

The user may name, then save the current eyepoint and center
of interest in the workfile. By subsequently selecting *[F7]›Get*,
the user can retrieve any previous eyepoint and center and
reproduce the viewing direction.

Displaying the Current
Eye-Center Coordinates

The current eyepoint and center of interest coordinates can be
displayed at any time by selecting *[F8]*.

PICTORIAL REPRESENTATION

The location of an object in a pictorial representation on a piece
of paper is often not apparent. A usual assumption is that the
object base is in the X-Y plane where Z = 0 but this assumption
is sometimes incorrect. Consider the box in Figure 14.17. Is its
base in the X-Y plane where Z = 0 or perhaps above the X-Y
plane? If the coordinates (5, -4, 0) of one of the points in the
base of the object is supplied, the location of the base is then
defined.

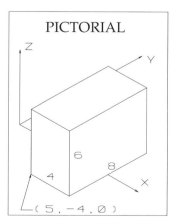

Figure 14.17

Another approach is to supply the top and front orthographic views of the object (see Figure 14.18). From the front view, it's obvious the box base is in the X-Y plane with Z = 0. Note that the top view shows the X-Y axes while the front view shows the X-Z axes.

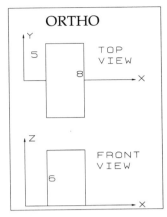

Figure 14.18

Keyboard Input

Instead of moving the cursor to locate objects, the user can key in coordinates. Select *[F1]›Absolute* or *[F1]›Relative* to enter X-Y-Z coordinates. Select *[F1]›Device* to return coordinate entry to the mouse or digitizer. For example, the given box can be added to the scene by selecting:

Add›Box›[F1]›Absolute›(5, -4, 0)
Relative›(4, 8, 6)

■ Menu Commands

[F1]›Device
    Absolute
    Relative

3D Database

A database is a set of data. From a database, the user extracts, sorts, modifies, and calculates selected data to produce a desired outcome. The U.S. census produces a database. From this database the Census Bureau extracts data to produce reports on such things as ethnic origins, business activity, population growth, and the number of bathrooms in an average three-bedroom residence.

Likewise, a 3D file is a database that consists of the following:

1. Object names

2. Object geometry (size, location)

3. Object properties (color, level, others)

4. Drawing features (preset rotation, tracking on, number of sides, others)

5. Other information (version number, number of objects)

When you select *Filer›Get*, the 3D file is copied to the V3D.WRK workfile. Data is then extracted from this workfile database, modified, and calculated to produce a display on the monitor screen. When you select a new viewing direction using *[F7]›Camera* or a new projection using *[F7]›Isometric* or *[F7]›Perspective*, the Vcad program uses the database data to calculate the new scene window display.

Pictorials Using 2D Methods

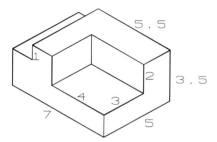

Figure 14.19

Here two ways to draw pictorials using 2D drafting methods for the notched block of Figure 14.19 will be reviewed.

Polar 2D: You could draw the notched box using polar coordinates. Figure 14.20 shows a partial path using this method. First select *Point (10, 5) Absolute*. Then select polar coordinates for the rest:

Angle	Distance
30	5.0
90	3.5
-30	-5.5
30	-5.0

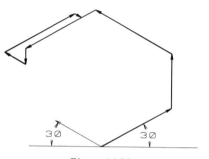

Figure 14.20

Group view 2D: You could draw the notched box using an orthographic partial top view. You could then select *Group›View›Copy›Top* to copy the top view in three layers (see Figure 14.21). You would then add, delete, and copy lines to complete the isometric.

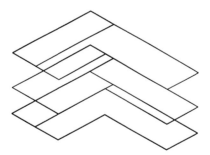

Figure 14.21

Pictorials Using 3D Modeling

Using *Modeling*, the notched box can be drawn in 3D as four adjacent boxes, then exported to 2D (see Figure 14.22). The unneeded lines are then erased to complete the drawing. Furthermore, once the database is established, any other view of this box can be exported to create another drawing of the object. Herein lies the power of 3D.

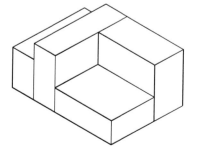

Figure 14.22

❏ DRAWING: VIEWS AND CHOICES

This drawing may require 1 mb of disk memory, an amount that is larger than the capacity of most floppy disks. The following instructions allow you to use the hard disk (C drive) as your current directory. The assumption is the C drive has enough free space to handle this (your instructor may have to verify this).

1. Key in the following:

Key In	Comment
C:	Use the C drive.
CD\	Change the current directory (CD) to the root directory. Use a backslash, not a forward slash.
MD $$$	Make a temporary directory (MD) called $$$ (which may already exist).
CD $$$	Change the current directory to $$$.
DIR	The first two lines will display the name of the current directory. If this name is $$$ and if $$$ contains files, key in DEL *.* to remove them. All but two files will be removed—on the screen these two files, part of every user-created directory, are listed as one point (.) and two points (..).

2. Keyboard input: Key in *Vcad*. Select *Modeling*. Select *[F6]›Sides›10*. Determine the coordinates required to locate the notched box, sphere, cylinder, and cone shown in the orthographic sketch in Figure 14.23. Use the measurements given in Figure 14.19 for the notched box (four adjacent boxes). Use *[F1]›Absolute* to enter the objects into the scene.

3. VIEW1: Select *[F8]* to display the default eyepoint and center of interest locations. Try to visualize whether the view is as expected based on this current eye-center viewing direction. Select *[F7]›Save›VIEW1›Quit* to save the default view direction.

4. VIEW2: With the center of interest still at (0, 0, 0), try to visualize what the scene might look like if the eyepoint were moved to (70, 30, 20). (With an X change from 50 to 70, there

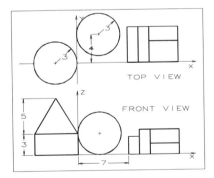

Figure 14.23

would be more of a right-side view. With a Y change from -50 to 30, the view would be from behind. With a Z change from 50 to 20, the view would be lower.)

Select *[F7]›Camera›Eye 70, 30, 20›Quit*. Using the [F7] menu, select *Save›VIEW2*. Test the changing of viewing directions by selecting *[F7]›Get›VIEW1*, then *[F7]›Get›VIEW2*.

5. VIEW3: Select *Camera›Center 2, 4, 3*, which places the center of interest at the sphere center. Select *Eye 2, 4, 70*, which places the eyepoint 70 units directly above the sphere. Does the view window appear as you expected?

6. Exporting: Select the following:

Quit›Get›VIEW1›Quit

Filer›Save›VIEWS (to save the 3D scene)

Export›Hidden›VIEW1

[F7]›Get›VIEW2›Quit›Hidden›VIEW2

[F7]›Get›VIEW3›Quit›Hidden›VIEW3

Quit›eXit Modeling›Keep

7. Library: The three different views will be displayed as a single drawing. Rather than attempting to use *Filer›Merge*, you will place the saved 2D drawings in a temporary library. Then you'll create an overlay, modify it, and finally plot it. This exercise provides more experience in working with a library.

Select *Library›dRive›B:›Make›VIEWLIB›3›Active›VIEWLIB* (this creates a three-symbol library called VIEWLIB). Select *Active›VIEWLIB*. Select *Symbol›Add›VIEW1*. Also add VIEW2 and VIEW3 to the library. *Quit* to LIBRARY, select *Overlay*, and create the overlay drawing with one row and three columns, unnumbered and with no titles.

8. VIEWS drawing plot: An overlay is a drawing that can be modified like any other drawing. Change the fat boundary to a thinner one. Add the titles VIEW1, VIEW2, and VIEW3. Add a border. Plot. Save as VIEWS (see Figure 14.24).

9. Export display choices: Exit *Drafting* and select *Modeling*. Select *[F7]›Get›VIEW2*. Then select *Export›Wireframe›WIRE* and *Export›Backface›BACKFACE*. Exit *Modeling*. Don't *Keep*.

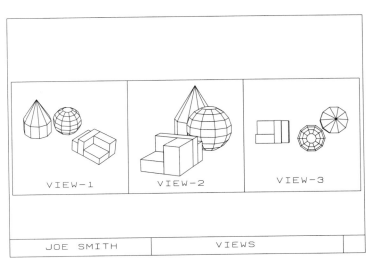

Figure 14.24

10. CHOICES drawing plot: Select *Drafting›Library›Active›VIEWLIB*. Select *Symbol›Delete*, then delete symbols 1, 2, and 3. *Add* the drawings WIRE, BACKFACE, and VIEW1 as symbols 1, 2, and 3. Make an overlay. *Add* the titles WIREFRAME, BACKFACE, and HIDDEN. Draw a border. Plot. Save as CHOICES (see Figure 14.25).

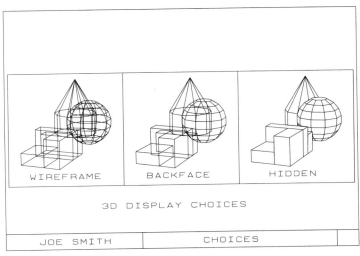

Figure 14.25

11. Removing the $$$ directory: Before removing the $$$ directory from C drive, you may wish to save it on a floppy disk (it may take more than one floppy). After saving to floppies, do the following:

Go to DOS, then key in DIR to make sure you're in the $$$ directory on C drive.

Key in DEL *.* to remove all files from the $$$ directory.

Key in CD\ to change to the root directory.

Finally, key in RD $$$ to remove the $$$ directory from C drive.

12. End of exercise.

CHAPTER 15

The 3D Create World

OBJECTIVES

- *To use the create world to create by extrusion, by sweep, and by creating surfaces.*

- *To move create world objects to the scene world.*

- *To make use of shaded drawings.*

CHAPTER CONTENTS

Introductory Concepts

Extrusion

Drawing: Extrusion

Drawing: Sweep

Adding Surfaces

Drawing: Shaded

INTRODUCTORY CONCEPTS

The objects placed in the 3D scene have been the primitives—box, cylinder, cone, and sphere—or combinations of them. Objects other than these primitives can be used, but they must first be created, then placed in the scene.

The **create world**, like the scene world, is three-dimensional. Objects are created in this world, then transferred to the scene world. The workfiles for the scene world and create world are different.

The **create window** displays a view of the create world. When the user selects *Create* from the SCENE menu, the scene window is cleared and the create window is displayed. The scene window is redisplayed when quitting from *Create*.

The Reference List for the create world at the back of this book lists the submenu for each menu item in *Create*. It also lists the *Create* function key menus. Although some menu items are the same as in the SCENE menu, many are different. We will examine a few of CREATE'S menu items to get a feel for the capabilities of 3D. Since a thorough knowledge of the menu items is required for mastering 3D, in-depth discussion is left for another text.

■ **Menu Commands**

Create›*Add*
       Modify
       Group
       Construct
       Filer
       Import
       Transfer
       Examine
       sKetch
       Scene

EXTRUSION

A number of common 3D objects can be drawn using a process called **extrusion**. An extruded 3D object is an object with an identical top and base; the edges that connect the top and base are all perpendicular to the top and base. A right cylinder is an extruded object. A cone is not. A vertical rectangle is an extruded object. A vertical trapezoid is not.

A 3D extruded object is formed by first drawing the base in 2D. While in 2D, each object that is part of the base is assigned top and bottom Z-coordinates, which will determine the elevation of the top and base when the base is extruded.

To prepare for the next drawing, at the computer examine the 2D menu choices for Z-coordinates:

[F6]›Zcoord

Modify›Properties›Zcoord

Group›Build›Props›Zcoord (does not work in version 5.3)

Group›Props›Zcoord (does not work in version 5.3)

Inquire›Objects›Props›Zcoord

When *Zcoord* is selected, the user is requested to key in the bottom elevation of the base to be extruded (usually 0) and the elevation of the top copy of the base. No change occurs in the 2D display; however, the *Zcoord* values are recorded in the 2D workfile.

■ Menu Commands

Create›Import›Get
Merge
List
Ext-list
dRive
Sides

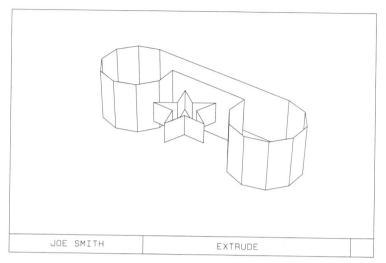

JOE SMITH   EXTRUDE

Figure 15.1

❑ DRAWING: EXTRUSION

Note: This drawing is shown in Figure 15.1. You should probably place the drawing close to the bottom left of the screen, since extrusion will take place from this origin. To extrude, you will select *Create›Import* from the 3D SCENE menu, then name the 2D drawing to be imported. Extrusion is automatic with the *Zbott* (bottom) and *Ztop* (top) values being used.

1. Execute Vcad and select *Drafting.* Select *[F6]›Zcoord›Zbott=0›Ztop=5.* Draw the left circle shown in Figure 15.2. Copy it to the right side. Draw the lines that join the circles and trim the circle.

2. Select *[F6]›Zcoord›Zbott=2›Ztop=4.* Draw the star by first drawing a pentagon. Draw the pentagon's diagonals. Trim and erase to form the star.

3. Move all objects close to the origin at the bottom left of the screen as shown in Figure 15.3.

4. Save as BASE.

5. 3D create: Exit *Drafting.* Select *Modeling›Create›Import› Sides=10.* Select *[control-F5]›Cursor* to set up the keypad for

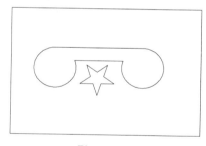

Figure 15.2

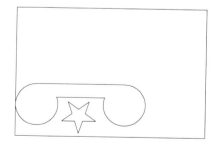

Figure 15.3

cursor movement. [Numlock] should be off. Select *Get›BASE›*
Z›Yes. The object is displayed in an exploded manner showing
each surface and the nodes (points) associated with each surface. If it is not centered, leave it that way. You can center it
later on. Select *F7›Render› Wireframe* (since new surfaces will
not be built, a wireframe display is more suitable).

6. 3D modeling: The object must be transferred from the
create to the scene world for further processing. The *Transfer*
menu item within *Create* is used to transfer objects from the
scene to the create world for modification, but we want to
transfer from the create world to the scene world. Therefore,
select *Scene*, lock the coordinates to (0, 0, 0), and select *Transfer›*
Merge›[enter] for all objects. Wiggle the mouse to display the
object, then record its location with the mouse button.

While staying on the X-Y plane where Z = 0, move the cursor
until it appears to be at about the center of the objects. Read
the coordinate display. Round the figures to the nearest in-
tegers and, using these values, change the center of interest.

7. Plotting: Select *Filer* to save as EXTRUDE. Then export to
2D as EXTRUDE. *Quit* from *Modeling* without *Keeping*. Select
Drafting›Filer›Get›EXTRUDE. Notice that the drawing shows
vertical surfaces only, there is no top or bottom. Put a border
around it.

8. Plot and submit.

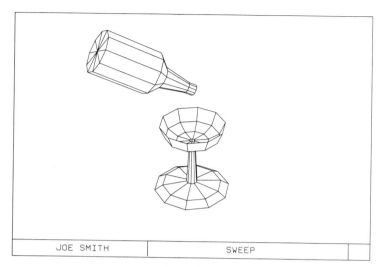

Figure 15.4

❑ DRAWING: SWEEP

The drawing shown in Figure 15.4 was created by importing a "wire" drawing to 3D, then sweeping. A sweep is a circular extrusion. Do the following:

1. Glass: Execute Vcad then select *Drafting*.

Select *Units›Base›*left: *0›*right: *15›*bottom: *0*. Draw lines as shown in Figure 15.5. Save as GLASS. Exit *Drafting*.

Select *Modeling*. Select *[control-F5]›Cursor* to set up the keypad for cursor movement. [Numlock] should be off.

Select *Create›Import›Get›GLASS*. Responses will be required for three Vcad queries:

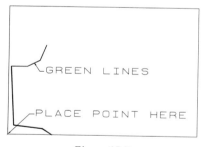

Figure 15.5

Enter the constant coordinate for projection: *X* (if X is constant, the GLASS wire drawing will be placed on the Y-Z plane).

Use Z-top and bottom values: *No* (we will not use Z-top or Z-bottom in this drawing).

Enter the constant coordinate value: *0* (the drawing will be entered on the Y-Z plane where X = 0.

Make the glass a group. Select *Group›Build›New›Yes›Properties› Color 3›Quit›Quit*.

From *Group, sWeep* about Z-axis 360 degrees with the number of wedges equal to 10.

Select *Create›Filer* and save as GLASS.

2. Bottle: Return back to the SCENE menu, then exit *Modeling.* Select *Drafting.*

Select *Units›Base›*left: *0›*right: *15›*bottom: *0.*

Draw the bottle wire as shown in Figure 15.6.

Save as BOTTLE. Exit *Drafting.*

Select *Modeling.* Select *[control-F5]›Cursor* to set up the keypad for cursor movement.

From the create world, import BOTTLE and sweep it.

Select *Create›Filer›Save›BOTTLE.*

3. Tilt the bottle: Select *Group›Build›New›Yes›Fence* and fence in the bottle. Quit to *Group.* Lock the coordinates at (0, 0, 0). Select *Rotate* and *Record* the pivot at (0, 0, 0). Select *X-axis›Angle›-45.* Select *Rotate* and *Record* the pivot at (0, 0, 0). Select *Y-axis›Angle›+45.*

4. Move bottle up five units: Select *[F6]›Increment›1›[enter]›Quit.* Select *Move›Find.* Place cursor at approximate middle of mouth opening. Pick, then quit. Unlock the Z-axis coordinate. Press [F4] to turn off tracking. Move cursor until Z = 5. Pick. *Quit* to *Create.*

5. Merge glass: Select *Filer›Merge›Glass›No.*

6. Move glass down five units: Select *Group›Build›New›Yes›Properties›Color›3›Quit›Quit.* Next select *Move›Handle›Find* and place cursor at the approximate bottom center of the glass. Pick and quit. With tracking off, unlock Z-coordinate. Move Z to read -5, then pick.

7. Move to the scene world. Transfer, then export to 2D. Make a border.

8. Plot and submit.

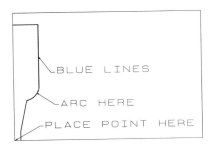

Figure 15.6

ADDING SURFACES

Objects in 3D have been developed in the create world by importing 2D objects, then extruding or sweeping. To create a 3D house, the walls can be developed by extrusion. However, the triangular peak of the end walls and the sloping roof present a problem, since they are not primitives, nor can they be extruded or swept.

Fortunately the *Create›Add* menu allows us to develop surfaces by creating nodes (points) in appropriate locations; the points are then joined by lines to form surfaces. The menu and sub-menu items associated with *Create›Add* are too extensive to cover in detail in this introductory text. However, our last exercise allows you to use *Create›Add* to create two surfaces, a top and a bottom, whose points have already been defined.

❏ DRAWING: SHADED

1. 2D drawing: Execute Vcad and select *Drafting*. Select *Units›Base›*left: *-7›*right: *7›*bottom: *-5.* Select *[F6]›Zcoord› Ztop=5›Zbott=0.* Create the drawing in Figure 15.7 in 2D. Leave out the dimensions. Save as RING. Exit *Drafting.*

2. 3D import: Select *Modeling.* Select *[control-F5]›Cursor* to set up the keypad for cursor movement. Select *Create›Import› Sides=10. Get›RING›Z›Yes.* Select *[F7]›Camera›Full›Quit›Quit* to increase the window size of the extrusion.

3. To 3D scene: Transfer the ring to the scene world. Select *[F7]›Camera›Full* to make it larger.

4. Initial shading: From the SCENE menu select *Display› Shade›[enter]* (no saving). Observe two problems. There is no top (or bottom) surface and the all-white display is too bright. From the SCENE menu, select *Filer›New* to clear the scene, then return to the create world.

5. Top surface: By grouping, make all edges red. There are eighteen points to connect to create a top surface. Recognize that some points are not clearly visible because they are hidden by the red edges. By inspection, locate (look at) all eighteen

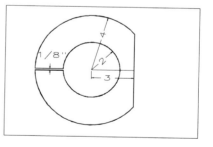

Figure 15.7

points. These points will have to be joined by lines to create a top surface.

Select *[F2]›Point* so the cursor will fix itself only on points.

From *Create*, select *Add›Surfaces›Type=18*. Pick all eighteen points: Starting at any point, completely traverse the top surface. The top surface will end up white because the preset color was not set to red.

6. Bottom surface: Make a bottom surface by selecting *Modify›Copy* and copy the top surface. The dashed (rather than blinking) object is copied. You may have to change handles to place the copy accurately. Make all edges red.

7. New shadings: Quit to the SCENE menu and transfer the ring. Don't worry about where it's placed.

After placing, select *[F7]›Camera›Full* if needed. Select *Display›Shade*. Save as SHADE1.

Select [F8] to examine eyepoint value. Select a new eyepoint to be able to see through part of the hole. Select *Display›Shade*. Save as SHADE2.

Make all edges green. Select *Display›Shade*. Save as SHADE3.

8. Macro: Outputting the fill areas of a shaded drawing might require more than a plotter. Rather than outputting, create a macro that allows screen observation of all three saved shade files.

From the MODELING menu, select [F9] and note the *D* (for definition) displayed at the bottom right of the screen. Then select the following:

Display›Display›Shade›SHADE1

Display›Display›Shade›SHADE2

Display›Display›Shade›SHADE3

[F9] (to end the macro definition)

Select *[control-F10]* to execute the macro. This new macro takes the place of a plot. Your instructor may wish to observe it.

9. From the SCENE menu select *Filer›dRive›G:DRAW›Get›* *BRACKET*. You won't lose your macro. The bracket is one of VersaCAD's 3D showpiece drawings. Select *Display›Shade›* *[enter]* (you will have to wait awhile before VersaCAD displays the drawings).

10. End of exercise.

More DOS

THE DIRECTORY

A **directory** is a file of filenames. Whenever a disk is formatted, a directory, called the **root** directory, is created on the disk. When a user saves a file on this disk, the name of the file, its size, the date, the time, and the file's location on the disk are recorded in the directory.

SUBDIRECTORIES

If a large number of files are stored on a disk, it is convenient to have related files grouped so that when DIR is typed, only the group of files of current interest are displayed. This grouping can be realized by placing each group in a different directory on the disk. Then when DIR is typed, the filenames in only one directory (the **current** directory) will be displayed. Other DOS commands will by default operate only on the files located in the current directory, unless otherwise specified.

The following DOS commands apply to multiple directories on a disk:

Command	Meaning
MD TEST	Make a directory. Creates a directory called TEST within the current directory. TEST becomes a **subdirectory** of the current directory. The current directory is the **parent** directory of TEST. Type DIR and the name TEST <DIR> will be displayed along with the other files in the current directory. A disk can contain 54 to 512 subdirectories, depending on the disk capacity.

CD TEST   Change directory. If TEST is a subdirectory of the current directory, then TEST becomes the current directory. Otherwise an error message is displayed.

CD ..   Change the current directory to the parent directory. The two periods are an abbreviation for parent directory. If the current directory is the root directory, then an error message is displayed.

RD TEST   Remove directory. Removes the subdirectory TEST from the current directory. TEST cannot be removed unless all the files in TEST, if any, have been deleted.

PATHNAMES

The structure of files in a directory is analogous to the structure of a family tree, with parent, child, and child with children resembling directory, file, and subdirectory.

The diagram in Figure A.1 shows how files on a disk in the C drive may be structured. The root directory contains the names of four files, two of which are subdirectories that contain files. Each file has a **pathname**, which essentially shows you how to locate a file within the directory structure (it shows you the path to the file). The pathname consists of the filenames of the directory and subdirectories that lead to the file you want; each name is separated by a backslash. In the figure, the bottommost name, ALICE, is stored in the subdirectory SAM, which is stored in the subdirectory GEORGE, which is stored in the BAKER directory, which is stored in the root directory. The list below contains pathnames for various files in the figure:

File	Pathname
ABLE	C:\ABLE
HENRY	C:\BAKER\HENRY
ALICE	C:\BAKER\GEORGE\SAM\ALICE

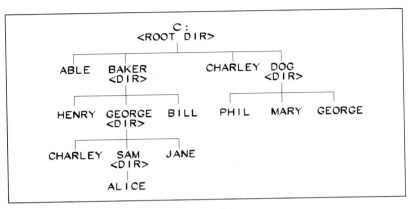

Figure A.1

The following abbreviations could be used for a file with the pathname C:\BAKER\HENRY.

Abbreviation	Comment
\BAKER\HENRY	Valid when the current drive is the C drive.
BAKER\HENRY	Valid when BAKER is a subdirectory of the current directory.

Pathnames are used to access, copy, rename, or delete files that are not in the current directory. The examples below (based on Figure A.1) detail some of these uses:

Command	Meaning
COPY BILL BOB	In the current directory, creates a copy of BILL called BOB.
COPY C:\BAKER\ HENRY C:\DOG	Copies the HENRY file to the DOG subdirectory.
DEL C:\DOG\ GEORGE	Deletes the GEORGE file in the DOG subdirectory.
DEL C:\BAKER\ GEORGE\JANE	Deletes the JANE file.
DEL JANE	Deletes JANE when GEORGE is the current directory.

THE WILDCARD CHARACTER

The star (*) character is a **wildcard** character that can represent characters in a DOS command. A wildcard character is convenient when a number of files are to be copied, removed, or deleted. The list below provides some examples:

Command	Meaning
TYPE ABLE.2D	Displays on the screen the file ABLE.2D in the current directory.
DEL ABLE.*	Deletes all files beginning with ABLE from the current directory. For example, this one command could delete ABLE.2D, ABLE.3D, and ABLE.2DL.
DEL *.2D	Deletes all files with the extension 2D from the current directory.
DEL *.*	Deletes all files from the current directory.
REN ABLE.* BAKER.*	Renames all ABLE files to BAKER.

BACKING UP A DISK

Floppy disks are inexpensive storage mediums. However, they are somewhat fragile: Their contents can be lost from too much heat (left in a car), rough handling (scratches), being near microwaves, or being dropped, sat upon, or bent. Your chances of losing your work are lessened if you periodically make a copy (a backup) of your disk so you have a duplicate. The process is relatively fast and the backed-up disk can be used again at the next backup session. Some students backup after every session at the computer station. But care must be taken—by mistake you could copy the older files over the newer files and lose your latest work.

The method of backup depends on the drive configuration. Assume the disk you wish copied, the source disk, contains no subdirectories. If your computer configuration is two floppy drives, do the following:

Place your source disk in A drive

Place your target disk in B drive

Type COPY A:*.* B:

If your computer configuration is only one floppy drive and a hard drive, you can use the hard disk as follows with the source disk in A drive:

C:	Makes the C drive the current drive.
CD:\	Changes the current directory to the root directory.
MD $$$$	Makes a temporary directory called $$$$.
CD $$$$	Makes $$$$ the current directory.
COPY A:*.*	Copies all the files in the A drive to the current directory.

Now remove the source disk from A drive and replace it with your target disk. Then do the following:

COPY *.* A:	Copies all the files in the current directory to the A drive.
CD . .	Changes the current directory to the parent directory. The user could also use CD\ since in this case the root directory *is* the parent directory.
DEL $$$$	Deletes all the files in the $$$$ directory.
RD $$$$	Removes the temporary $$$$ directory.

If you are backing up on a regular basis, you can create a batch file to speed up the above process. Refer to batch files in the DOS manual.

The 2D Mode Display Area

Five rectangular areas are used on the monitor screen when VersaCAD is executing in 2D (see Figure B.1): the menu area, the graphics area, the message area, the mode area, and the coordinate area.

A mode is a manner, form, fashion, condition, or arrangement. In the mode area of the monitor screen, VersaCAD displays the current state of seven different modes (see Figure B.2). A letter indicates which state any given mode is in. If none of the states of a given mode are currently active, a period (.) is displayed.

The names of each mode together with the meaning of each mode letter are described below:

1. Input: Change the mode state by using *Input* or [F1].

    D   Digitizer

    K   Keyboard

    M   Mouse

    A   Absolute

    R   Relative

    P   Polar

2. Snap: Change mode state with [F2].

    I   Increment

    G   Grid

    O   Object

    .   None

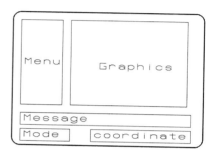

Figure B.1
MONITOR SCREEN AREAS

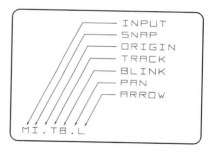

Figure B.2
MODE EXAMPLE

3. Origin: Change state with [F3].

      O   Shifted origin

      .   Default origin

4. Tracking: Change state with [F4].

      T   Tracking on

      .   Tracking off

5. Blinking: Change with [control-F4].

      B   Blinking on

      .   Blinking off

6. Pan multiplier: Change by pressing the [insert] key, then a digit (numeric multiplier).

      M   Multiplier on

      .   Multiplier off

7. Arrow keys: Change with [control-F5].

      C   Cursor text editing on (user must also select *iNput›Keyboard*).

      L   Display list pan/zoom feature on.

      S   Scroll on. C is displayed if scrolling is not supported.

Alphanumeric. Consisting of alphabetic characters or digits.

Aspect ratio. The ratio of the height to the width of the monitor screen.

Attribute. Same as *property*.

Base. The width of the graphics area in world units.

Boot. Cold boot: The computer powers up after having its power turned on. It sets parameters, makes diagnostic checks, and then turns control over to the operating system. Warm boot: Same as cold boot except the power is already on; the user presses [control-alt-delete] to initiate a warm boot.

Bug. A malfunction in the hardware or software.

Byte. A storage location unit, used to measure the size of stored information. One character uses one byte of storage. One kilobyte equals 1,000 bytes; one megabyte equals 1,000,000 bytes.

CAD. An abbreviation for computer-aided drafting. Sometimes means computer-aided design.

Command. A set of computer instructions within a program whose execution is usually initiated by the user. DIR is a DOS command. *Modify* is a VersaCAD command.

Coordinate. In VersaCAD 2D drafting, a pair of numbers used to locate a point. The X-Y coordinates (3, 5) locate a point three units horizontally and five units vertically from the origin. In 3D, the coordinates of a point are a triple of numbers locating a point in the X, Y, and Z directions.

Absolute coordinates: The X-Y or X-Y-Z coordinates of a point as measured from the origin. Contrast with *relative coordinates*.

Relative coordinates: The X-Y or X-Y-Z coordinates of a point relative to a reference point, usually the previous point.

Polar coordinates: A pair of numbers (not X-Y numbers) that angularly relate a point with a reference point, usually the previous point. The first number is the angle formed from the reference point as vertex, the positive X direction as the first leg, and the segment from the reference point to the desired point as the second leg. The second number is the distance from the reference point to the desired point.

World coordinates: See *world*.

Coordinate display. The small rectangular area in the lower right corner that displays the coordinates of the cursor.

CPU. An abbreviation for central processing unit, the circuitry that cyclically fetches, decodes and executes instructions from main memory allowing the computer to operate.

CRT. An abbreviation for cathode ray tube, a televisionlike device used to display alphanumeric and graphic output.

Crunch. To remove unneeded information from a datafile. A workfile is crunched when information that has to do with erased objects is removed.

Cursor. A flashing bar, small box, or plus symbol displayed on the screen to locate the current point of interest.

Database. A set of data. From a database, data are extracted, manipulated and calculated to serve a specific purpose. The workfile is a database. Data are extracted, manipulated, and calculated to form a drawing on the CRT.

Default. An initial value, condition, or state of a part of a system, which is not determined by the user. Contrast with *preset.*

Digitizer. An input device that can sense the location of a probe within a rectangular area.

Directory. A file of filenames. A file containing the names and location on the disk of a set of files.

Display. To output on the monitor screen.

Disk. A circular object whose area can be magnetized to store information.

Floppy disk: A thin circular sheet that can be inserted into a disk drive so that information can be stored on or retrieved from it. The sheet can flop around within its protective cover when it is not inserted and spinning.

Hard disk: A not-so-thin, more rigid disk that is usually permanently built into the drive. The hard disk has more than ten times the capacity of a floppy disk. It is also more than ten times as fast and more than one hundred times as expensive.

DOS. An abbreviation for disk operating system.

Drive. An electromechanical device with read-write heads used to handle disks.

EGA. An abbreviation for enhanced graphics adaptor, which is the circuitry that receives and transforms information from the CPU into signals that are sent to the CRT screen in a 640-by-350 pixel count form.

Entity. An *object* or a *primitive.*

Execute. To cause a set of computer instructions to be performed.

Explode. To change a record in polygonal form to linear form. When an existing pentagon is exploded, its single polygonal record is converted to five linear records.

Factor. A numerical value that defines the size change of an object or group of objects from their original form to their enlarged or reduced form. An object that is double size has been enlarged by a factor of two.

Fatlines. A form of display that is related to the width of objects. If fatlines is off, all objects are displayed as *width 1* objects. If fatlines is on, an object is displayed at its current width.

Feature. Any peculiarity; anything specially prominent. An object has arrow, marker, and template features. A display has units, grid, and all-level features.

File. A set of information stored outside main memory, usually on a disk. A file is sometimes considered a location outside main memory where information can be or is stored.

Fillet. An arc joining two nonparallel lines. A corner-rounding feature.

Floppy disk. See *disk.*

Font. A set of characters whose elements are distinguishable by their characteristic form. Old English and Gothic are examples of fonts.

Format. To create storage locations on a disk so that information can later be placed in these locations. When a disk is formatted, all previous information on that disk is destroyed.

Function key. A key on the keyboard that is marked with an F and a number from *1* to *12*. Function keys can be programmed to perform a particular function (set of instructions) within a program when the key is pressed.

Graphics area. A rectangular area on the monitor screen that is used by VersaCAD to draw objects.

Grid. A series of horizontal and vertical dotted lines whose equally spaced dots aid the user in precision drawing.

Group. A set of objects whose elements contain some characteristic which separates them from other elements.

　Current group: The group most recently formed by using *Group›Build.*

Handle. One of a set of predefined points on an object. Also a point located by the cursor and used to move, copy, image, rotate, or scale an object or group of objects.

Hard copy. Paper output from the computer.

Hard disk. See *disk.*

Hardware. The devices of a computer system. Contrast with *software.*

Hatching. To draw a set of parallel lines or a pattern within a given area.

Increment. A distance preset using *[F6]›Increment.* After *[F2]›Increment* is selected, the cursor will jump the preset increment rather than move smoothly across the screen.

Input. Information received by the computer from input devices. The keyboard, the mouse, and the digitizer are input devices.

Kilobyte. See *byte.*

Layer. Same as *level.*

Level. An alternate graphics display that can replace or be merged with the current graphics display. Each existing object is assigned a level number. When its level is turned on, the object is displayed.

Library. A file containing drawings that are symbols and may be used as objects in the current drawing.

Macro. A set of instructions that can be executed as though they were a single menu item.

Marker. A plus symbol centrally located within an object. A marker may be displayed or left undisplayed. In dimensioning, a marker is a symbol (an arrow, a slash, or a backslash) placed at the ends of a dimension line.

Megabyte. See *byte.*

Monitor. The output device that contains a CRT.

Mouse. An input device that is moved around on a pad or surface. Mouse input information translates to cursor movement.

Multiline. A set of parallel lines that may be drawn as though they were a single line.

Object. A primitive or a symbol.

Operating system. A program that controls the input-output activity of the disk and of other peripheral devices. The operating system executes until it moves an application program from the disk to main memory. It again executes when the application program has completed its task.

Origin. A point from which absolute coordinates are measured. Initially the 2D origin is at the lower left corner of the graphics area. The 3D origin is initially at the center of interest.

Output. Information sent by the computer to an external device. The CRT and the plotter are output devices.

Overlay. A drawing containing rectangular areas, which is used with a stylus on the digitizer to select menu items, library symbols, macros, and cursor location.

To merge with other objects. To place over.

Pan. To view panoramically. To move the viewing window so as to see other drawing or scene areas.

Parameter. A variable.

Peripheral. An input or output device.

Pick. To select or record by pressing the mouse button.

Pixel. An abbreviation for picture element. A spot on the screen that can be activated by the CRT's electron gun.

Plot window. The rectangular area containing the objects to be plotted.

Plotter. An output device that produces on paper the contents of the plot window.

Polar. See *coordinates*.

Preset. To change the default settings.

Primitive. A relatively simple geometric figure that is used in combination with other primitives to form more complex figures.

Program. A set of computer instructions.

Prompt. A symbol on the screen that requests user input. A forward (>) symbol is the DOS prompt. VersaCAD uses a colon (:).

Property. A color, pen number, style, level, or any other element of an object's record.

Real world. Same as *world*.

Record. The set of elements required to uniquely define an object. The elements of a 2D object are its record number, object number, geometric coordinates, color, pen number, width, style, visibility, level number, groupname, density, and its top and bottom Z-coordinates.

To complete the record of or change the record of an object. The recording action is either the final pick or the final press of the [enter] key.

Relative. See *coordinates*.

Resolution. The precision of detail on a CRT screen, usually measured by the pixel count in the X and Y directions.

ROM. An abbreviation for read-only memory, that portion of main memory whose byte content cannot be changed. ROM is not erased when the power is turned off.

Scale. Same as *factor*.

Scene. The volume used to locate the set of three-dimensional objects to be drawn.

Select. To choose a menu item.

sKetch. To redraw the objects currently in the graphics area.

Snap. To use the [F2] function key to locate a point.

Software. The information (programs and data) stored and used by the computer system.

Stylus. A pencil-like device containing a wire coil, used to move the cursor and to make picks on a digitizer.

Symbol. A drawing that has been placed in a library.

Template. The number 8 linestyle for an object.

Toggle. To move to the other state of a two-state condition. The user might toggle between *Yes* and *No* for *Fatlines*. Toggle may also mean to select the next state in sequence of a multistate condition. For example, the user often toggles through the dimension markers.

Tracking. Prior to recording an object, to change its size, shape, and location corresponding to the movement of the cursor.

   Tracking line: The line that is displayed from picked point 1 and that temporarily uses the cursor location as point 2 until point 2 is picked.

Viewing window. A rectangular portion of the world as seen in the graphics area of the monitor.

Workfile. A file containing the records of existing objects as the drawing is being created. The contents of the workfile are eventually saved in a file with a .2D extension.

World. The area (2D) or volume (3D) used to locate objects to be drawn.

World coordinates: The coordinates displayed in the coordinate display area in the lower right of the screen.

Z-coordinate. The third-dimensional component of an object's location.

INDEX

REFERENCE LIST FOR VERSACAD DESIGN 3D
SCENE WORLD SUBMENUS

ADD	MODIFY	GROUP	FILER	EXPORT	DISPLAY	TRANSFER	SWITCHES	UNITS
Box	Find	Build	dRive	dRive	dRive	Merge	All levels	Units
Cylinder	<backward					Objects	Levels	Wireframe
cOne	>forward	Move	Get	Wireframe	Illuminat	Wireframe		
Sphere		Copy	Save	Backface	Shade		Keyboard	
	Delete	Rotate	Merge	Hidden	Hidden		Hidelines	
Wireframe	Undelete	Scale	Delete	Orthograph	Display		Wireframe	
	Properties	Image			List			
			New	Delete				
	Move	Delete	List	List	dRive			
	Copy	Undelete	Ext-list	Ext-list				
	Rotate	Properties						
	Scale		What					
	Image	Active	Pause					
		eXhibit						
	Wireframe	Wireframe						

FILER:	Scene World	⟷	3D File	
EXPORT:	Window	⟷	2D File	
DISPLAY	Scene World	⟷	3D Shadefile	
TRANSFER:	Scene World	⟵	Create World	

INPUT	CREATE	VIEWPORT	INQUIRE	WIREFRAME	BACKFACE	EXIT
Device	Add	Add	Object			Yes
Keyboard	Modify	Remove	Group			No
Overlay	Group		Increment			Keep
Alt menu	Filer	Get	Zero			
	Import	Save				
	Transfer	Delete				
	Examine	List				
	sKetch					
	Scene					

F1	F2	F3	F4	F5	F6	F7	F8	F9
Input	**Snap**	**Ref/Org**	**Track**	**Cursor**	**Preset**	**Window**	**Current Eye-Center**	**Define Macro**
Device	None	Origin		Short	Level	Camera		
Absolute	Increment	Reference		Labeled	Color	Isometric		
Relative	Grid	Trace		Long	grpName	Perspective		
	Object				Increment			
					Grid	Get		
					Rotation	Save		
					Density	List		
					Sides	Delete		
						Wireframe		

ctrl-F1	ctrl-F2	ctrl-F3	ctrl-F4	ctrl-F5	ctrl-F6	ctrl-F7	ctrl-F8	ctrl-F9	ctrl-F10
Clear	**Resnap**	**Screen**	**Blink**	**List**	**Freeze**	**Cpl**		**Macro**	**Execute**
Keybd					**Coord**	**Input**		**Menu**	**Current**
		Text		Cursor	**Display**				**Macro**
		Command		dispList				Save	
		System		Inquire				Delete	
				Home				List	
				Zoom inc				dRive	
								Execute	